Risk

RISK

An Introduction

Jakob Arnoldi

polity

First published in 2009 by Polity Press

Polity Press
65 Bridge Street
Cambridge CB2 1UR, UK.

Polity Press
350 Main Street
Malden, MA 02148, USA

ISBN-13: 978-0-7456-4098-3
ISBN-13: 978-0-7456-4099-0(pb)

A catalogue record for this book is available from the British Library.

Typeset in 10.5 on 12 pt Sabon
by SNP Best-set Typesetter Ltd, Hong Kong
Printed and bound in Great Britain by MPG Books Ltd, Bodmin, Cornwall

The publisher has used its best endeavours to ensure that the URLs for external websites referred to in this book are correct and active at the time of going to press. However, the publisher has no responsibility for the websites and can make no guarantee that a site will remain live or that the content is or will remain appropriate.

Every effort has been made to trace all copyright holders, but if any have been inadvertently overlooked the publishers will be pleased to include any necessary credits in any subsequent reprint or edition.

For further information on Polity, visit our website: www.polity.co.uk

Contents

Acknowledgements

This book is the result of research undertaken between 1998 and 2007. Listing all the people from whom I have received help in that period would be an impossible task, so grateful thoughts, of which there are many, will have to suffice. As for the writing of the book, a much more recent enterprise, Ulrich Beck, Anders Blok and Christian Borch have provided many valuable comments on various drafts, and I thank them sincerely. I have had numerous discussions about risk, capitalism and uncertainty with Scott Lash, Michael Keith and Tyler Rooker. The readers at Polity Press have provided constructive and knowledgeable criticism which has greatly improved the manuscript. Students in Munich and Copenhagen have endured seminars on risk in which I have presented what at times were only half-baked (or less) arguments. Jens Ludvigsen and Louise Barner have helped me to get hold of the articles and books that have travelled across my desk during the last twenty-eight months. Sharon Kirsch has been a diligent proofreader, and has added thoughtful comments on the content as well. Finally, the staff at Polity Press have been a pleasure to work with; their professionalism has been much appreciated.

Writing this book coincided with the first two years of the life of my son Max. The parallel tasks of writing a book and parenting have caused stress and sleep deprivation, for me and for my wife, to whom many thanks are due. It has been a pleasure writing this book, and a joy watching Max grow and develop. This book is dedicated to Max and Cecilie.

1
Introduction

Risks are social

Risks are potential dangers. We are all confronted with risks every day, and we all have well-developed skills with which we constantly assess the various risks and how best to avoid them – or rather reduce them the best we can. No matter how hard we try, risks cannot be avoided. We constantly accept and/or take risks because accomplishing anything necessarily entails risks of all sorts: a choice of career means the risk of not fulfilling one's goals and ambitions, using any mode of transportation means the risk of accident, falling in love means the risk of heartbreak. We take and avoid risks both consciously and unconsciously. We perhaps consciously tell ourselves not to quit a job we dislike because it would be risky to do so before having found another one. We do not drive round a bend faster than we (most often subconsciously) believe is safe, and maybe we shy away from an attractive possible partner because we find it just too risky to place all our emotional stock in that person. Or conversely, sometimes we enjoy driving just a little too fast, or congratulate ourselves on having succeeded in a risky career move, or seek the thrills of a new and uncertain love affair.

But risks are not just problems that we have to deal with individually. *Risks are social*, which is the starting point of this book. Briefly, three reasons can be mentioned: risks are social and political *problems* – for example, the problem of creating an ecologically sustainable society; risks are understood against *a social and cultural background*, that is, people worry about different risks due to different social and cultural backgrounds; and risk is a key concept in various *practices* and *knowledges* with which people are governed and society is structured. For instance, systems of social insurance are social institutions built around knowledge of risks.

The three reasons are taken from arguably the three most important sociological theoretical approaches to risk.

1. The first approach, best represented by the work of Ulrich Beck and Anthony Giddens, takes as its point of departure new dangers from modern technologies and the way in which scientists, politicians, the public (laypeople) and the mass media experience immense difficulty coming to terms with these risks, because they are complex and surrounded by uncertainty, because of their potential magnitude and because they upset our ideas about what is natural and what is not. Resulting problems are lack of trust, lack of solid ground on which to make decisions and, above all, fierce political struggles over who is responsible and what should be done politically.
2. The second approach is that of Mary Douglas and her collaborators, which focuses on the cultural logic behind the marked differences in what people fear and which risks they are ready to take. Some people worry more about, say, the risks of global warming, while for others terrorism is a much graver risk. All individuals fear for their lives and health, but they nevertheless hold different beliefs about risks and manage them differently, and they do so not at random but rather according to specific social and cultural logic.
3. The third approach is taken by scholars inspired by Michel Foucault's notion of governmentality. Here the focus is on how risk is used in various technologies of government and on the power that risk can hold over people. I mentioned social insurance as a social institution that is based on ideas and knowledge of risk. Obviously the concrete design of social insurance has considerable influence on how society is structured. A

different example could be how modern medicine screens patients to establish risks – for instance, screening foetuses for Down's syndrome. Yet another example, also related to health, could be the information campaigns launched by governments to influence public behaviour. Such information is often about risk – of smoking, being obese and so on. The examples might seem very different, but the thing they share is that knowledge of risks is used to govern citizens.

As indicated, these three approaches translate into three of the main sociological theories of risk that are described in chapter 3 of this book. But the three are not exhaustive of sociology of risk. Another key area of study could be voluntary risk taking – for instance, engaging in extreme sports – and there are several others.

Risk in contemporary society

Risks have not always been problems high on the political and public agenda, and they are not used as technologies for government the same way today as they were fifty years ago. As for problems, one of the first instances where a new awareness of technological side effects emerged was the discovery that heavy use of pesticides in agriculture severely damaged the health of humans exposed to them. Today such health concerns are commonplace: worries abound about radiation from mobile phones, the side effects of genetically modified (GM) technologies, carcinogens in food and phthalates in children's toys, to name but a few. At the same time, global warming poses severe threats to society. For several reasons, these risks can be said to be of a type that until the late 1960s hardly existed. They are often unknown to laypeople without information from scientists. Somewhat paradoxically, they are nevertheless surrounded by uncertainty, as scientists often have difficulty describing the magnitude of the risks with even an approximation of certainty. Many of the risks – for instance, global warming – are furthermore potentially disastrous and would, if they were to materialize, radically change both society and nature. And, lastly, they are all unwanted and unintended side effects of technological progress; they have as such led to new debates about what constitutes progress and whether social and economic progress through technological innovation is sustainable. Globally as well as nationally, society faces a range of problems that are caused by human efforts to forge a better and more efficient society.

In roughly the same period that these concerns about the risks of technology emerged, many Western societies started to embrace uncertainty in new ways. The rolling back of welfare state provisions and the rise of neoliberalism diminished the social safety net for many people and made the labour market more volatile. This has made life more risky for many people in terms of career, life planning, access to social insurance and perhaps even identity and sense of self (Bauman, 2000; Sennett, 1998). Yet this is far from the only reason for the sociological interest in these social changes. Risk also plays another role, and a significant one, in this development. The reason is that the political changes have to a large extent been brought about by political and economic theories that have rethought notions of risk and uncertainty (and the distinction between them – see below). Neoliberalism has explicitly argued for a need for people to become more entrepreneurial, based on economic theories that describe entrepreneurialism as uncertain risk taking that is essential to the creation of wealth. Neoliberalism attacked, and continues to attack, the model of the welfare state not only because the costs are deemed too high but also because too much security against risk suppresses individual entrepreneurship and responsibility (see O'Malley, 2004). These political changes which have valorized uncertainty have not meant, however, that the concept of risk is no longer used by governments to plan and to make decisions. On the contrary, risk is used in all sorts of government; more and more state regulation is built around scientific concepts of risk (Rothstein, Huber and Gaskell, 2006).

Ulrich Beck has famously suggested that modern society has become a risk society, as reflected in the title of his 1986 classic. Beck's groundbreaking book took new technological risks as its point of departure, and in the foreword he deals with the nuclear disaster at the Chernobyl plant that happened in April 1986. Beck's book more than anything else rendered risk an object of sociological study. Since then, other sociological approaches to risk have appeared – for instance what I will call the governmentality approach, which has been at the forefront of the study of the changing function of social insurance and redefinitions of risk and uncertainty. There are many differences and disagreements between these theories (and several other mutually conflicting theories). However, one central thesis does unite the various theories – the idea that since the late 1960s or early 1970s risk, in various guises, has come to play both bigger and new roles in society. In this book I shall adopt the term 'risk society', using it to refer to the various roles risk plays in contemporary society. The premise will be that fundamental changes have occurred in most Western, and arguably all industrial, societies since the early 1970s and that risks play several roles, both new and augmented, in these fundamental changes. Many social theorists, including theorists of risk, have difficulties with the idea of big social changes that mark a transition from one epoch to another. There are valid reasons for questioning the idea of epoch-making changes. Risk plays several new roles in modern society, and one should not assume that these new roles all are driven by one underlying cause or that these roles are the same in all parts of the world. Yet some fundamental, and by and large synchronous, changes are visible, and these I intend to outline.

The three approaches outlined above show a perhaps worryingly broad approach to risk in sociological research. In the first approach, the risks of technology feature heavily, while risk in the third approach is not so much risk *of* something or some action as it is risk as a concept that could be used *for* different (governing) purposes. That the sociological notion of risk is so broad – fuzzy, in fact – might be seen as a weakness. But this fuzziness is inevitable precisely because the key insight into risk that sociology has delivered is that risk involves more than simply an objectively given probability.

The kinds of risks analysed by sociologists are in many cases potential dangers, such as pollution, environmental disaster, pandemics, terrorism, war and conflict, or financial instability (Beck, 1999; 2007). But the list expands beyond a list of 'bads'. David Garland presents arguably the most concise and comprehensible list of the forms of risk analysed in sociological analysis:

> Risk is a calculation. Risk is a commodity. Risk is a capital. Risk is a technique of government. Risk is objective and scientifically knowable. Risk is subjective and socially constructed. Risk is a problem, a threat, a source of insecurity. Risk is a pleasure, a thrill, a source of profit and freedom. Risk is the means whereby we colonize and control the future. Risk society is our late modern world spinning out of control. (Garland, 2003: 49)

Garlands's list captures effectively the spectrum of sociological research on risk. All of these definitions of risk will be described at length in this book, but it might also be worth explaining briefly here what is meant. Sociologists are generally wary of the idea that risks are calculable and hence objective, but they are interested in *objectifications* of risk – that is, how such calculations are made and what they are used for. Insurance, both private and public, might make for the most prominent example. Another could be finance, where such calculations of risk have created financial markets in which risks are traded, rendering risk a commodity and a kind of capital. Creating and managing such things as social insurance systems is, as has been said, a way of governing society. Investigating how risk is calculated, objectified and used often exposes how risks have been objectified differently at different times, and how such objectifications serve different interests and are shaped by values and culture. This means that risks are socially constructed (I return to this below). Obviously risks are often a source of fear, as they are potential dangers, but, as mentioned above, some practices such as extreme sport can also be seen as deriving their meaning from the very fact that they are risky. Likewise, the idea of entrepreneurialism, much celebrated in contemporary society, is essentially about taking risks or braving uncertainty. And the new class of risks caused by technology undermines the hope for technological progress and human control.

The (un)reality of risk

In the years leading up to the new millennium there were widespread concerns about whether or not electronic devices containing microchips would continue to function after midnight 01.01.2000, because many such microprocessors (so to speak) were only configured to keep track of time in the twentieth century. There were fears that everything from coffee machines to the global financial system to nuclear reactors would malfunction if they were not made 'Y2K ready'. Concerns were voiced in the mass media, and huge amounts of work-time and money were invested in making sure that the new millennium would not start with a technological disaster. As it turned out, nothing serious happened, perhaps because the concerns were unfounded, perhaps because technicians had foreseen the problems and taken the correct measures. Y2K was soon forgotten.

Y2K is one example of great concern about future or potential dangers, and also an example of how these concerns by no means always materialize. In the risk society risks are anticipated and precautionary measures taken. On the other hand, history provides many examples of new technologies that were celebrated as great innovations, only for severe side effects to be discovered later. When the chemical company Du Pont invented chlorofluorocarbons (CFCs), it was not known that their use in the production of refrigerators, among other things, would cause dramatic ozone depletion, which in turn has caused increased ultraviolet (UV) radiation, which then in its turn has caused alarming increases in the rate of human skin cancer, among other things. As a matter of fact CFCs were for a long time celebrated as being harmless. Past experience of such things, and the painful experience of the continuing effects today, have arguably created a public frame of mind in which fears of possible negative side effects of new technologies are a knee-jerk reaction. But it is not only laypeople who react instinctively. Steadily accumulating scientific knowledge means that various negative side effects – or, in many cases, possible negative side effects – have been exposed.

Science also creates knowledge of potential dangers in another way. Today it is possible to conduct genetic screening for a range of diseases, meaning that 'patients' (a term that is acquiring a new meaning because the people in question actually are healthy) can obtain prognoses about the likelihood of their developing diseases later in life. Discovering a high likelihood then might lead to prophylactic surgery; for instance, given the increased likelihood of breast cancer, patients may choose to have prophylactic mastectomies. As in the cases above, potential dangers are pondered and calculated, and precautionary measures are taken.

The underlying paradox of this discussion is of course that the risk society is not necessarily a more dangerous society. Life expectancies are generally rising in Western societies. Risks are not *actual* but rather *potential* dangers. Among other things, their impact on contemporary society is due to the fact that many risks – for example, nuclear accidents – would be on a catastrophic scale if they were to occur; moreover, they are surrounded by scientific uncertainty that causes problems not only for scientists but also for decision makers who have to act on inconclusive scientific reports. Risk has an impact, too, in the medical arena. While medical knowledge about potential dangers, sophisticated prognostication techniques and prophylactic treatment indeed extend people's lives, being told of an 80 per cent risk of developing cancer in later life nevertheless has dramatic impact.

It is difficult to worry about everything in the future. Our perception of which risks are most serious is to a wide degree influenced by our cultural values and world views. Most of us have probably experienced how others hold different perceptions of the direst risks. Risks are viewed differently simply because people adopt different beliefs about the world, and a significant reason for these differences is cultural background. It is also easy to see that problems such as environmental risks are politically contested and that opinions about risk tend to be distributed along existing political lines. If a person is right-wing, it is less likely that she or he will be concerned about the risk of nuclear energy, for example. The opposite is the case if the person is left-wing.

As another example of the importance of values, let us imagine that a new drug against cancer has been discovered.

The drug works well in most cases, extending patients' lives by many years, but 10 per cent of all patients experience severe heart problems due to the drug, from which 5 per cent die. Is this an acceptable risk? Most people would probably say no, but how low does the probability have to be then? Most people would probably agree that the drug does not have to have zero risk for its use to be accepted, given its benefits. But where, then, is the acceptable threshold? Answers to that question have to be based on ethics and values; probability does not do it alone – indeed a mere figure might be seen as insufficient.

Two imagined scenarios involving risk

The first imagined scenario regards responsibility, values and knowledge. Let us imagine that I was suddenly, on only a slightly overcast day, struck by lightning. If that did happen, probably no one would say that I had taken an unnecessary risk (or that someone had exposed me to such a risk). But then imagine another scenario in which I chose to stay during a thunderstorm under a tall tree on a high hill with a long metal pole in my hands. If I were then struck by lightning, some people would probably say that I had taken a stupid risk. Likewise, if someone had told me to stay under the tree holding the pole, that person would probably be blamed for having exposed me to risk. The difference between my two invented scenarios turns on whether I or someone else can be held responsible for my mishap, based on knowledge of risk factors (causes and effects). If there is no one who can be held responsible, we would probably all see the mishap as pure chance, as bad luck, as a naturally caused accident.

Risk more or less disappears in the latter scenario. In other words, risk is the opposite of pure chance, because it involves human agency. For the same reason it is also the opposite of random acts of nature. What we often refer to as natural causes is something that suspends human responsibility – no one is responsible. But when humans can be held responsible, risk emerges. We can assess the risks and try to manage them, and blame can be attributed to those who have managed the risks badly or exposed others to risk. And note that we do so based on knowledge of cause and effect. If we did not know that lightning strikes high structures and is attracted to metal, it would not have mattered where I had stood or what I had held – the event would, in any case, have been seen as a random act of nature and as bad luck.

The attributability of risk, its relationship to decisions and actions and its reverse relationship to nature and randomness, is tantamount to saying that risk is social. To assess when one can speak of natural causes and when blame can be attributed relies on human values. As such, risk is subject to change as human values change, and it can be negotiated and challenged. Even if I had chosen to stay under a tree on a hill with a metal pole in my hand, I might just about have been able to justify my actions by pointing out that the risk of doing so is still statistically much lower than, say, the risk of driving a car on average 30 miles a day. By drawing on that knowledge I would literally be able to show that I knew what I was doing – that I was acting responsibly (just for the record: there are a lot of data on the risks of driving a car and being hit by lightning, but none for the specific risk of being struck by lightning while standing under a tree on a hill holding a metal pole, so the example is imaginary). In a religious community I could furthermore have possibly defended my actions by pointing to my blind faith in God. In other words, exposing oneself to unnecessary risks often invokes moral condemnation, but one might also use values to legitimize one's actions. Another example of how questions of risks are negotiable would be the increasingly hostile attitude to smoking. Part of this hostility is fuelled by the argument that smokers expose themselves to unreasonable risk, and often the moral undertone is inescapable. Yet the same argument is rarely used against, say, people skiing or mountain climbing or drinking. What is deemed risky depends not only on objective risks but also on values. The example also shows that risk involves being held to account. We are faced with the prerogative of being responsible for our actions on the basis of knowledge and values. Implicitly the question hovers: why did you stand there with a metal pole in your hand? Or why do you smoke? And because of such questions we conduct ourselves accordingly; that is, we do not act grossly irresponsibly. Given this influence on human behaviour, risk is a way of exerting power.

With the proliferation of human technology and the new class of risks stemming from these technologies, the scope of human actions and human decisions has drastically increased. Humans know much more about the natural world and, thanks to technology, they can manipulate things much more effectively. Therefore more can be attributed to human actions and decisions. Take flooding as an example. When floods occurred, say, two hundred years ago, they were probably seen as more or less random acts of nature or maybe as a sign of God's will. Nowadays there is little that is pure nature. Rivers are regulated, drainage systems are installed and weirs and levees are built. Therefore most floods can and will be attributed to bad decisions and inadequate engineering and technology, in this case inaccurate calculation of the maximum water pressure or failure to build levees high enough. In most cases there are good reasons for this, but clearly the boundary between what is nature and what is human responsibility can be hard to establish. And more human factors stack up all the time. To stay on the topic of flooding – today another factor has emerged, namely global warming. Floods today can therefore be attributed not only to bad engineering but also to extreme weather caused by carbon dioxide emissions that are the result of human activity.

Obviously the increased technological scope affects general values and perceptions of where random nature ends and human responsibility begins. For example, increased technological scope arguably creates a simple feeling that humans are to blame, indeed that we ourselves are to be blamed for our own misfortunes. Think about health. In contemporary society the attitude predominates that we can all assume responsibility for our own health by eating well, taking adequate exercise and so on. Moreover, these values are actively ingrained in us through information campaigns mounted by health authorities – campaigns in which information about risk features heavily. Most people today know which foods are good for us and which are not. By means of such information, humans are made responsible for their own conduct.

The reader might have noticed that this last issue offers an example of how risk is used as a technique of government; we are given information about risk to change our conduct. Earlier in this chapter I referred to this as the third of three main sociological approaches to risk. The two other approaches have in fact resurfaced as well – the first in the discussion about the increased scope of technology, and the second in the discussion about human values and responsibility.

The second imagined scenario indeed calls for a bit of imagination. Imagine that anything could cause everything, that anything might be possible. If that really was the case, no one would be able to do anything for fear of what might happen. One would not dare to carry out even the most mundane actions, such as turning on the television, for fear that it might cause the boiler to explode or the sun to darken. The floors might not carry weight and therefore not be safe to walk on. Luckily, when it comes to most things in the real world, we have relatively certain expectations about what causes what and what does not. We know that turning on the television is relatively safe and that floors are mostly even, have no holes and will hold our weight. This set of expectations without which we could not exist is based on previous experiences. So far, no one has turned off the sun just by turning on the television, so we can be pretty sure that this will not happen, and having walked on many floors makes us expect smooth and stable surfaces. However, when it comes to new technologies, past experience might not grant us the same certainty. Indeed, past experience might even tell us that things indeed interact in ways not originally foreseen. Above I mentioned CFCs, which are a good example of a new technology first being celebrated as effective with no side effects, only for severe side effects to be detected later. This kind of experience hinders us from forming stable expectations, or perhaps it leads to us forming expectations that try to take into account the unexpected.

'Expectations that take into the account the unexpected' is a rather strained expression, so instead I suggest that we talk about broad frames of expectations. Something – let us use CFC gases as an example – is understood to have a series of possible effects, good or bad. Each of the individual effects may not be fully known, but at least there is an outline of the worst and the best that might occur. This is the frame of expectations. It is the same with turning on the television – we might include among our expectations that television can destroy eyesight or provide great entertainment, but no worse or better than that. When CFCs were invented, it was known that chemical substances could be poisonous or otherwise damaging, so these possible consequences were included in the frame of expectations. CFCs were celebrated as harmless precisely because these expectations of possible negative side effects proved unfounded. On the other hand, the possibility that CFCs might cause skin cancer through a complex causal chain – CFCs to refrigerators to ozone layer to UV rays to human skin – was not included in the frame. Today, however, when faced with new technologies, one may frame the possible effects of new technologies much more broadly than was the case at the time of the invention of CFCs. Based on knowledge of the past, one can worry about a wide extent of possible negative impacts from a given new technology. And the reason for these negative projections is precisely the knowledge of earlier cases in which the initial narrow framings were shown to be inadequate.

More importantly, this insecurity about where the list of possibilities should end creates room for many *different* expectations about the possible pros and cons of new technology. For example, debates about GM foods show that this issue is often being framed differently. Citizens have expressed a wide range of concerns about the possible effects of GM foods. Some might be tempted to say that certain of these concerns are the product of overly vivid imaginations, but, even so, differences in framing occur also in scientific studies. Should the possibility of insects carrying GM pollen and thus polluting fields with non-GM crops be included in the frame of possibilities for scientific risk assessments of genetic modification technology? How many possibilities can be justified scientifically as plausible possibilities that must be taken into consideration?

In sum, problems regarding risks can be framed differently. If the problems are framed narrowly, only a selected array of possible cause-and-effect relationships will be taken into consideration, often based on strict criteria of scientific knowledge. If the problems are framed broadly, many possible relationships will be taken into consideration, based on more lax criteria. As has been said earlier, framing of some kind is necessary. No framing – the inclusion of all possibilities – would mean fear of carrying out even the most mundane of actions because the world might fall apart as a result of doing so. The relevant distinction is hence between narrow and broad framings. Framing issues broadly means assessing risks less rigidly, for example, including so-called unknown unknowns (see chapter 5) in the assessments of such possible risks.

The dilemma is that there are no easily defined answers as to how widely the issues should be framed. Science might have methodologies and standards, and in society in general we certainly have strict, although implicit, ideas about what can rationally be expected and what not. But scientists also constantly disagree about the exact framing, as do laypeople. In the end, and this is by now becoming a trivial point, values as much as anything else influence how issues are framed.

The sociological approach to risk

Risks are social, I wrote. Sociological approaches to risk are distinct from what can roughly speaking be called the probabilistic and the psychological approaches to risk. In the majority of the natural sciences and in economics, risk is most often defined as the probability of an event, in many cases further calculated by multiplying the probability factor with a numerical measure of the extent of the consequences. A wealth of statistical data on risks have been accumulated, so that knowledge exists of the probability of accident when, say, flying or driving a car. Combined with assessments of the extent of the consequences – expressed, for instance, as the economic costs of car accidents or air crashes – risks can be calculated. This is the basis for the actuarial technique used in the insurance industry.

Another way of approaching risk is psychological (in the field of risk research, this is also known as the psychometric approach). Here the focus is on the psychological factors that trigger fear and uncertainty and that therefore magnify the 'objective' risks. Risks with extremely dire consequences

– for instance, the risk of nuclear disaster – tend to score high in laypeople's risks assessments, even though the 'objective' risk is low compared with other more mundane risks – for instance, the risk of a car accident. The objective risk is of course defined statistically. Researchers within the psychometric tradition argue that the reason why subjective assessments see some risks as graver is that risks such as those of nuclear accident have what is called a high 'dread factor' (Slovic, 1987; Slovic, Fischhoff and Lichtenstein, 1979). The dread factor is an emotional factor that 'distorts' the perception of risk.

Seen from a sociological perspective, such psychological research on risk confirms that there is more to risk than mere probabilities. But most sociologists are at the same time critical of the psychometric tradition's distinction between 'objective' and 'subjective' – for two main reasons. First, such a distinction strongly implies that the objective risks are real and rational, while the subjective risks are the misguided irrational conceptions of laypeople (Strydom, 2002: 79). Many sociologists would argue that such subjective perceptions cannot be reduced to irrational beliefs and that such beliefs, for example, mirror deeply rooted moral concerns about the potential capacity of human technology to destroy, say, the global ecosystem. The second sociological objection, which also draws on the role of norms and values, is that the values that shape people's perception of risk are not so much subjective as inter-subjective. That is, they are cultural as much as they are psychological (see chapter 6). In spite of these differences between a psychological and cultural approach to risk the psychometric approach is not irrelevant, and cross-disciplinary research drawing on both sociological and psychological theory has been undertaken with great success. One such example, which we shall encounter later in chapters 6 and 7, is the idea of social amplification of risk.

To employ a much used and abused term, most sociologists can be said to take a social constructionist approach to risk. The basic tenet is, first, that human knowledge and understanding are influenced not only by whatever it is that is being known or understood – that is, reality – but also by culture and meaning. Second, the idea of social constructionism often (although not always) entails a strong focus on power and the discursive processes in which reality is constructed. The powerful tend to have the biggest say in how things are understood and known, and there is a great deal of power in being able to influence how reality is known and understood. There are great variations in how radically these points are made (Gergen, 1998; Hacking, 1999; Sismondo, 1993; Turner, 1991; Velody and Williams, 1998), ranging from the idea that the culture and meaning *influence* the perception of reality to the argument that culture and meaning *determine* our conception of reality. Such variations can also be found in sociologies of risk, as we shall see later in this book.

This book

This book aims to provide an introduction to the various sociological approaches to risk. The term 'sociological' calls for a caveat. Exactly where the boundaries lie between sociology and related disciplines such as ethnography or anthropology, not to mention 'disciplines' such as science studies and cultural studies, can be hard enough to gauge under normal circumstances; when it comes to the study of risk, setting the boundaries is even harder. Studies of risk tend to traverse disciplinary boundaries, no doubt because risks often involve technology, politics, nature, culture, cognitive schemata and many other phenomena that the traditional divisions of academic labour try to keep separate. Not surprisingly, the study of risk is often a trans-disciplinary exercise; risk is a central theme in new hybrid fields of study such as science and technology studies (STS), and theories of risk challenge traditional sociological theories. So the term 'sociological' is used in a very loose sense indeed.

The bulk of the chapters (4 to 9) are built around the key themes in the literature, such as environment, science, technology, health, culture, mass media, risk taking, politics and power. The two preceding chapters are, however, different. Chapter 2 presents a genealogy of the concept of risks which goes beyond the use of risk in the social sciences. The aim is, in other words, to convey a sense of how the idea of risks has been used and is being used today. With modernity, ideas about risks became cornerstones of modern science, social reforms and other technologies of government. Knowledge of risk was used to manage and distribute risks, which helped to materialize the great emancipatory ideals of modernity. Given this connection between risk and modernity, it is not surprising that *late* modernity has seen new technologies of government in which the ideas of risk are recast. Out of these changes also springs the sociological understanding of risk sketched out in this chapter.

Chapter 3 introduces the main sociological theories of risks: the theory of reflexive modernization, the cultural theory of risk, and the governmentality tradition. In many ways the introduction of these theories sets the scene for what will be discussed in the following chapters. Other theories are also mentioned, and in several cases are dealt with in more detail in the following chapters.

Then comes a string of chapters with a thematic structure. Chapter 4 addresses technology and nature. Modern society is permeated by complex technologies, and many risks are potential and unintended side effects of these complex technologies. Complexity also means unpredictability. Technology moreover radically alters nature and, above all, changes, and disturbs, human ideas about what nature is. These ideas about nature are in turn important because they greatly influence how we comprehend risks. Crudely put, opposition to risk often equals opposition to something that humans conceive of as unnatural.

Chapter 5 deals with science in the risk society. The role of science in the risk society is paradoxical – and in more ways than one. On the one hand, it is most often due to scientific knowledge that we know about risks, yet scientists often disagree about exactly what it is we know. Moreover, the technologies that pose risks are often created thanks to scientific 'progress'. For this reason, the public often views science with scepticism. Yet at the same time we are all exposed to scientific knowledge and forced to respond to, and act on, scientific information both in our mundane everyday life and in times of crises. When we go shopping, for instance, we bring along knowledge about why organic foods might be less risky, and we know why food with a lot of saturated fat is unhealthy. In times of crisis – for example, when seeking medical help – we are increasingly asked to make active choices about treatments. Science is everywhere, and no one can avoid encountering it and acting on a basis of scientific knowledge. As a consequence, we are being 'responsibilized'; knowledge is being heaped upon us with the expectation that we alter our conduct accordingly.

While we may know, say, which foods are healthy and which not, we often do not act in strict accordance with this knowledge. People have vastly different habits and preferences when it comes to choices and actions to avoid risks, and different people interpret scientific information differently. Such differences are cultural, which is the topic of chapter 6. Perceptions of risk, it is argued, cannot be separated from cultural values, and both science and politics are influenced by culture.

Cultural perceptions about risk are to a large extent shared by social groups and even societies. They are shared because they are communicated, and communication increasingly takes place via the mass media. The mass media can at times give skewed accounts of the risks because they are better equipped to deal with some types of risk than others. And at any given time there are some risk issues that receive a lot of attention while others are more or less ignored. Chapter 7 is devoted to analysing the inner logic of mass media and its consequences.

Risk does not always entail potential dangers that must be avoided. People also sometimes seek risks – for instance, when they undertake extreme sports where an element of risk gives them a buzz. Once again, the role of culture is crucial here; cultural convention dictates which risks it is legitimate to seek and which not. The risk society, I argue in chapter 8, has seen a large-scale renegotiation of this normative framework, with individual or *private* risk taking being more valued and *public* risk sharing being devalued. It is no coincidence that 'private' and 'public' are used here. This is not only a cultural change but also a political change, spearheaded by neoliberalism, which values private entrepreneurialism (risk taking) over public welfare provision (risk sharing).

This political shift is only one of the political roles that risk plays. Chapter 9 deals with risks and politics, and with the government *of* risks and government *with* risk. When it comes to risk, the political does not merely consist of how risks should be managed and what constitutes a fair distribution of risks. Risks are ambiguous, and perception of risk depends on values and culture. Hence the very definition of risk becomes political. Risks such as global warming cannot be contained by individual nation states but require supra- and transnational collective action. This poses a range of problems, but also the possibility of a radical redefinition of politics and solidarity that goes beyond nationality and nation states. Finally, various conceptualizations of risk lead to specific forms of government – government with risk, as I just called it. Neoliberal policies are one example of specific conceptualizations of risk leading to specific policies, but concepts of risk are used throughout many strands of government, and not just in regard to big political programmes and ideologies.

Chapter 10 is the concluding chapter. It argues that the theme of risk and social inequality has to some extent been neglected in the literature so far. Finally, it is suggested that the risks facing contemporary society create both new openings and new closures. On the one hand risk necessitates, and creates, new forms of cooperation and a new sense of solidarity. On the other hand, risk also creates new forms of power, best witnessed in initiatives to address the risk of terrorism, which suppress civil liberties and exclude and punish those who are deemed to pose risks. Perhaps the very future of modernity balances on risk.

2

The possibility of Hume: a brief genealogy of the concept of risk

Hume has become possible

Foucault, 1970: 60

And Hume thereby became possible

Hacking, 1975: index of chapters

Risk and modernity

In 1748 the Scottish philosopher David Hume published *An Enquiry Concerning Human Understanding*, in which he offered a since-famous critique of inductive reasoning. Roughly speaking, induction is the forming of expectations about the future based upon past experience; we assume that the sun will rise tomorrow based on the experience that it has done so every morning until now. Inductive reasoning is often based on concepts of causality as described above: based on knowledge of causal relations, we can predict, say, that passing one's hand through the flame of a candle will cause pain. Simply put, inductive reasoning is the forming of expectations based on past experience. But induction not only has to do with causation, it also has to do with probability. As we shall see later in this chapter, with the developments of modern science, the expectations or predictions entailed in induction came to be developed by means of probability

(Daston, 1988: 202; Stove, 1973: 38). Probability is a scientific method used to make scientific assertions about uncertain matters. Probability made it possible to induce the chances of something happening in the future. This is the cornerstone of the modern concept of risk: the scientifically (probabilistically) calculated likelihood of something unwanted happening.

Hume's critique is a historical marker in at least three ways: only from about fifty years before Hume had science become probabilistic and inductive. Of course people have always made inferences about the future based on knowledge of the past. But science was until the seventeenth century based on ideas of demonstrative proof and classifications. But at that time a scientific and probabilistic form of inductive thought emerged and with that, of course, a scientific concept of risk. It was this rise of inductive thinking from the mid-seventeenth century onward that made Hume (or rather his critique of induction) at all possible, as Foucault and Hacking assert.

The second way in which Hume's critique is a historical marker is that Hume was not advocating a move back to old science with its focus on classifications and proofs; he was simply sceptical of *determinist* induction, arguing against determinism. It was, in other words, not induction per se but the very deterministic flavour which inductive thinking had at the time that drew Hume's criticism. The idea at the time was that the world was governed by stable causal laws which could be uncovered by inductive and probabilistic thinking. The significance of Hume lies in the fact that he foresaw that modern science in the coming centuries would continue to use inductive reasoning, and probability, but would become much less determinist.

Third – and this is the reason why I start this chapter with his critique – Hume's critique was the starting point of a long discussion about what can be determined and what not. Can we humans by means of our intellects, our knowledge and science foresee and hence control the physical world? If we to some extent can, is it at all desirable or will it quell human creativity and entrepreneurialism? And if we cannot, is it then a very dangerous illusion because it means that we create technologies under the false assumption that we can foresee their effect on the environment? Such questions have, in various guises, been debated ever since. This means that the concept of risk has since Hume's time had an important role not only in science but also in politics and society in general.

This chapter gives a broad account of how the idea of risk has evolved – and been used – through time. There are three reasons why such an account might be valuable. The first is the basic one that risk, while a relatively new concept in sociological theory, is an old concept in many other strands of life and in other parts of academia. Knowing some of this historical background is helpful in order to understand the concept as it has been employed in sociology.

The second reason is that the concept of risk has helped to shape the understanding of what human life and human society are about and how they should be governed. As we shall see later, the idea of risk has had an important role in the conceptualization of society as a governable entity. Correspondingly, changing ideas about risk bring changes to how humans understand themselves and society. For example, new ideas about risk and risk taking have fundamentally altered the political landscape in recent decades, with neoliberalism stressing the need for more individual entrepreneurial risk taking.

The third reason is that there is a tendency, if at times only implicitly, to link risk to modernity and late-modernity. Crudely put, the link was created as follows: before modernity humans did not know of risk, but instead thought of possible misfortunes in religious terms, that is, as acts of god(s). With modernity, humans came to see themselves as masters of their own destiny, hence they became interested in calculating the likely outcome of their actions which the concept of risk made possible. With late-modernity, humans have lost faith in their own ability to calculate the risks and master their own destiny – humans are left with neither religion nor science.

There is indeed a link between risk and modernity, but care needs to be taken when understanding it and such a careful understanding is the main aim of this chapter. As argued by Giddens (1999: 22), for example, modernity entailed a break away from the past and a much more strategic view of the future. Modernity meant much more deliberate collective and individual action with the aim of shaping the future according to human will. Central to this was scientific knowledge about risk, which could be used to intervene in and engineer both nature and society; for example, creating government institutions and programmes such as social insurance schemes could shield citizens from future dangers, that is, *risks*. The idea of risk helped to construct the concept of society as an entity which could be governed by humans.

Scientific calculations of future uncertainty are synonymous with the invention of mathematical probability theory. Probability theory, which started to emerge in the 1650s, signified a wholly new and powerful way in which humans could deal with uncertainty, and it became a cornerstone of the scientific developments of the industrial age. Probability made it possible to produce scientifically based estimates of things that were uncertain. For example, the precise outcome of a roll of dice cannot be known with certainty, but probability allows for an estimate of the chances of all the given possible outcomes. But probability can be used to predict much more than the possible outcomes of a roll of dice. As we shall see later, it can be, and is, used to predict, monitor and engineer many things in both the physical and the social world.

Like many others I shall ultimately argue that risk is intrinsically linked to modernity, but at least two caveats need to follow such claims. First, even if they did not have a developed calculative or conceptual apparatus at hand, (pre-modern) humans before the invention of probability were of course also trying to manage, distribute and diminish risk, both as discrete individuals and as societies. Anthropological work, including that of Mary Douglas, which we shall examine in the next chapter, shows how all cultures at all times have had (varying) conceptions of risk and various ways of managing and sharing risks (Bollig, 2006). Diseases could and can strike humans, their livestock and their crops. Storms, droughts, earthquakes, war, violence and other human disasters could and can wreak havoc on human societies. Moreover, risks and disasters were previously and are also today intertwined in a cultural cosmology through which blame is laid and responsibility attributed. In that sense, little has changed. The future can spring some nasty surprises, and humans have always invested considerable effort in foreseeing and avoiding the worst of these, and blaming others when they did not succeed. And even though risk as an idea to a large extent *is* modern, it is not the case that the concept of risk suddenly emerged during the Enlightenment. Humans already understood both risk and probabilities rather well before formal mathematical theories were invented (Franklin, 2001: 330).

Second, it is not the case that a scientific concept of risk was suddenly discovered and has remained unchanged ever since. Scientific notions of what is calculable are to some extent historically contingent, and they often have political connotations, as we shall see later (chapter 9). This is only underscored by the fact that within the last thirty to forty years risk has arguably attained a meaning other than calculable or probabilistic risk. Risk has come to mean that which cannot be calculated and that therefore is uncertain.

For these two reasons at least, an account of risk needs to start before the advent of modernity, and it needs to avoid some simplistic ideas about sudden changes in how humans have dealt with risk. The most simplistic interpretation of the differences between modern and pre-modern understandings of risk would presume that in the pre-modern world view the future was opaque and only the gods knew what lay in wait for humans. Accordingly, accidents and disaster had to be accepted as god-given misfortunes. Pre-moderns may have sought out oracles or read signs to get some idea about what the gods had in store for them, or they may have made sacrifices or prayed for a less risky future. Yet they also carried out actions that seem more logical from a modern viewpoint – and they did so on the basis of ideas about risk. Take insurance as an example. Insurance, we shall see later, is today fully dependent on probabilistic risk calculus, but primitive forms of insurance could also be found in antiquity and even earlier. For example, primitive forms of futures contracts date back to the Byzantine world of 2000 BC (Swan, 2000: 28). Such contracts specified future deliveries of grain to ensure that both buyers and sellers could feel certainty about the price of a future transaction; hence the contracts were a form of insurance. According to François Ewald (1991) the Italian 'risco' means 'that which cuts' in reference to cliffs and reefs, which potentially could sink ships and put human lives and cargo at risk. It is no coincidence that Ewald, a pre-eminent historian of insurance, mentions ships and seafaring. In Greek antiquity sea voyages would be 'insured' by high-interest maritime loans that were repayable only if the ship and cargo made it safely to their destination. If one lender made several such loans, he could offset the losses of one loan with the extra money generated by the high interest from the repayable loans, and a primitive insurance system would thus be in use. Underscoring this, the 'interest rates' varied according to season (Franklin, 2001: 259), that is, they varied according to the probability of storms and rough weather. Franklin's point is that even though the ancient Greeks were unable to calculate mathematically the correct insurance premium, they did have conceptual understandings of risk and the correlating interest. Risk assessment does not have to be mathematical.

In mediaeval Europe the economic calculation of risk often conflicted with the Church, which banned usury (taking interest on loans). Hence the forms of sea cargo insurance just mentioned were banned by papal decree in 1237 (Daston, 1988: 117). The explicit reason why the insurance was not banned earlier was that the Church in principle banned passive profiting from money lending but did not ban economic risk sharing (Franklin, 2001: 263, 68). It was legal to earn a profit from investing money in a venture (hence taking a risk), but illegal to give a loan demanding the return of the money plus interest in the event of the venture's failing.

Daston (1988: 19–20) speculates that bans such as the 1237 decree on economic activities were a major incentive for developing formal new ways of calculating risk – forms of calculation that could conceptualize risk in such a way that risk sharing could be separated from taking interest. Daston's argument might be an exaggeration, but it shows that risk is always entangled in definitional struggles involving beliefs, moral values and politics. The fact that maritime loans were deemed to be risk sharing until 1237 shows that judgement

vidual could embark on adventures which, given the necessary skills and strength of character, could bring great rewards.
This romantic idea of the adventurer had its origins in
eleventh-century notions of chivalry, but two centuries later
it gave rise to a more economically based idea of adventure,
linked to seafaring merchants. In both of its forms, the
notion of adventure places much emphasis on agency, on
the adventurer. This contrasts with earlier tales of adventures,
such as Homer's *Odyssey*, where Odysseus was fully in the
hands of the gods. Bonß uses this development of the idea of
adventure to show that there was no sudden shift from godly
Fortuna to individual virtue, but rather a slow progression
where individual agency – and with it, causal impact
and responsibility – came more to the fore. From this we
might also conclude that throughout the history of mediaeval
Europe a tension existed between the two notions of adventure, a tension that among other things would manifest itself
through discussions about risk taking and usury (something
that we saw above was indeed the case). Bonß illustrates this
by referring to changing interpretations of the legend of
Phaeton, the son of the Greek sun god Helios, who tried to
steer his father's sun chariot but could not control the horses,
fell towards earth and was destroyed by Zeus. Originally,
this legend was a tale of transgressing the boundary between
the human and the divine. But in the course of time the legend
changed, Bonß claims, so that increasingly *the causes* of Phaeton's fall were outlined and the means by which a
recurring accident could be avoided was discussed. A
move towards what we might, tongue in cheek, call technology assessment (in this case, of sun chariots!) thus slowly
began, with detailed analyses of the causes of previous
accidents.

Bonß arguably creates too strong a distinction between
modern ideas of risk taking and pre-modern religious ideas
of divine fortune – a misconception that I have tried to steer
clear of. But he also points to an increasing emphasis on
individual agency, meaning that the autonomous person
increasingly came to be seen as the master of her or his own
fate rather than as a puppet manipulated by fortune. In a
slow historical process, risk becomes internalized – something

linked to human agency rather than random nature. One consequence of this, which we shall return to several times later in this book, is that the future dangers become risks and rendered governable (Ewald, 1993b: 226). Bonß, however, ignores an important point: pre-modern humans, even though they perhaps believed events to be in the hands of fortune, nevertheless sought to shield themselves against *mis*fortune through such means as primitive forms of insurance. Thus it is not correct that there were no conceptions of risk at all. Bonß nevertheless rightly points out that cause and effect came to play much more important roles in thought, a development which is also present today. A central feature of modern scientific reasoning is precisely the idea that the future is caused by the past or, more to the point, that inferences about the future can be made based on knowledge of past events.

Probability

For most sociologists the word 'probability' has connotations of statistical laws and determinism, but probability is in fact Janus-faced (Hacking, 1990: 2). On the one hand, the laws of probability reveal the regularities in nature and society, an example being the bell curve. On the other hand, probability also has to do with uncertainty. Probability can be a means for guessing the odds or it can be used to describe the random or near-random behaviour of various phenomena, for instance, quantum behaviour in physics (Krüger, 1987). For risk, probability is of course important because it makes possible assertions about the likelihood of future dangers (an inductive process). Probability, one might say, turns future uncertainty into a scientifically known risk (although it is worth not subscribing fully to this analytical distinction; see chapters 8 and 10).

The French mathematician Blaise Pascal is normally credited with the invention of probability, but the fact is that around the year 1660 several people were starting to think about it (Hacking, 1975: 11). Gambling generally played a big role in the development of early probabilistic theories. So, by the way, did something else that seems odd today – namely legal questions about the truthfulness of witness statements (attempts to fathom such truthfulness mathematically have since been abandoned and replaced with conceptual notions of probability; see below).

One of the early breakthroughs in probability theory was the so-called Bernoulli's theorem. Bernoulli was able to express mathematically how the size of a sample relates to the precision with which one can make assertions about the total population. Odd as it may seem, this had a causal interpretation for many years: probability was held to express the degree of truth value of statements regarding the causal laws of nature (Gigenrenzer et al., 1989: 28). This early modern scientific world view was deterministic; it assumed the physical world to be governed by hidden but powerful laws of cause and effect. This was precisely the idea about which Hume was sceptical.

Probability theory was not at first used to calculate risk in relation to insurance and other economic assessments of risk. Indeed, until the nineteenth century life insurance was illegal in most European countries because it was considered to be a form of gambling. Quite incomprehensibly for us today, life annuities were on the other hand legal (and not considered gambling). Life annuities were contracts that entitled the buyer to an annual payment either for a specified number of years or, most commonly, for the rest of the buyer's life. The buyer of an annuity would in others words bet (at least so it seems from the modern perspective) that he or she would live long enough to receive more money back than constituted the purchasing price of the annuity. Let us set aside discussions about whether or not this was gambling. The point is that by and large probabilistic knowledge was not used for the pricing of the annuities, or for the pricing of insurance policies in the rare cases when these were allowed, until the nineteenth century. Indeed, only on rare occasions did the age of the buyer affect the price of the annuity (Bernstein, 1996: 87; Daston, 1988: 119–42)!

The understanding and application of probability did, however, change in the centuries after Pascal. In today's terms, early probability was by and large subjective probability (or perhaps one should say that objective and subjective probability were conflated). What this means is that nature was not held to behave randomly; rather, the source of uncertainty was incomplete human knowledge of the laws of nature. Probability was hence used to assess the probability of human knowledge being true. Slowly, however, a distinction between objective and subjective probability began to crystallize. With these developments, new applications for probability theory emerged and old ones withered away. Legal theory abandoned numerical probability theory, turning instead to conceptual understandings of subjective probability, most notably the idea of proof beyond reasonable doubt, with which anyone who has seen a court drama on television is familiar. This is worth noting because it also shows that non-numerical ways of working with probability and uncertainty exist and have been formalized in and adopted by the institutions of modern society. At the same time, new ideas about objective probability were integrated into the natural sciences, above all in physics (Krüger, 1987). This led to a gradual but radical change – from Newtonian theories of the laws of cause and effect and steady trajectories of matter in time and space to a theory in which natural matter is held to behave randomly. When this is the case, lack of human knowledge is not the cause of uncertainty, random nature is. Physics and other natural sciences started to use probability to understand dynamic (that is, changing and evolving) physical systems. Many of the great discoveries of nineteenth- and twentieth-century physics – for example, in the field of quantum mechanics – utilized probability theory.

In the context of this book, however, the most significant development was that the separation of subjective and objective probability also led to the emergence of statistics, that is, data on observed frequencies of events which with probability could be used for inductive extrapolations regarding future development or larger populations. Ian Hacking links this to the development of objective probability, asserting that the new-found indeterminism in nature and other phenomena led to an interest in the distributions and frequencies of natural and social phenomena, a statistical re-taming of the newly discovered chance (Hacking, 1990).

Risk, statistics, government – the discovery of society

Statistical techniques fuelled a whole range of new forms of government. In Hacking's own words, an avalanche of numbers led to the creation of new and powerful ways whereby the state could govern. Scholars from the governmentality tradition have shown to great effect not only how the state acquired new technologies of government but also how the very object of government – the population – was created through statistical monitoring of it (O'Malley, 2004). Risk played no small role in this process. Insurance, and that means first of all social insurance, became one of the prime ways in which the modern state was able to provide social security for its citizens. Such new forms of governing were possible because risk had become mathematized. The newfound statistical regularities in both natural and social phenomena made probabilistic calculus of risk, and hence insurance, possible (Ewald, 1993a: 173). Or, as Gigenrenzer et al. assert,

> The relationship between belief in statistical regularities and confidence in insurance was a symbiotic one: those who could persuade others of the existence of such regularities pointed to the financial success of insurance companies; insurance companies in their turn considered every new such regularity (e.g. between sunspots and epidemics) to be support for their practices. (Gigenrenzer et al., 1989: 182)

This new understanding of risk, based on knowledge of statistical distributions of events and the ability to make prognoses and risk calculations, also had another effect: when risks are no longer due to chance but are rather subject to human knowledge, they also cease to be purely natural. Nature might behave unpredictably, but once humans have the ability to fathom this behaviour, nature also becomes a social and political problem. François Ewald has in a series of publications described this as an internalization of risk (Ewald, 1991; 1993a; 1993b; 2002). Up till the middle of the nineteenth century, he asserts, disaster and accidents were attributed to nature and seen as more or less random. However, industrialization and the accidents it brought with it, along with the new insights into the statistical distribution of random events, changed that. Industrial work exposed workers to accidents no matter how careful or responsible the workers were. And statistics made visible the unequal distribution of the risk of having accidents. Consequently such accidents ceased to be seen as natural and thus external. Instead they become *internalized*, that is, they came to be seen as *social* problems.

Classical liberalism, which was the dominant mode of political and legal thought in the nineteenth century, saw misfortune as random acts of nature that responsible and prudent individuals could avoid. But towards the end of the nineteenth century these notions of random nature and individual responsibility gradually gave way to what we might call social liberalism, which put much more emphasis on risks as social problems. In other words the notion of risk as a social problem and the idea of the state as caregiver and insurer, so to speak, insinuated themselves between the notions of random nature and individual responsibility, in the end unsettling this axis of classical liberalism. Consequently a whole new way of conceiving of causality and the relationship between humans and society emerged. The idea that there could be *social* causes arose.

This, according to Ewald, was the beginning of the welfare regimes in European societies. Ewald puts risk at centre stage of this development, linking it to insurance and thence to the development of welfarism. Solidarity came to replace individual responsibility, and liberalism was replaced by social liberalism. Ewald even claims that the notions of risk and probabilistic reasoning became the compromise in the struggle between capitalism and socialism that raged in many European countries during the nineteenth century. But it is important to note that this new role of risk extends beyond welfare provision per se. In the course of the twentieth century, risk evolved from a concept in insurance to a general social category, a general concept for the scientific objectification of all sorts of social problems ranging from crime to health.

It is difficult not to relate to modernity the development Ewald describes so eloquently. The notion of calculable risk and the internalization of risk as a social problem, which the state can manage through insurance (thanks to risk calculations), is closely related to the emancipatory ideal of modernity, that is, the ideal that humans, through science and knowledge, would master the forces of nature and create a better and more just society.

Risk, then, entails a strong belief in the ability to calculate, a strong belief in the objectivity of these calculations, a strong belief in the utility of such calculations and, of course, a strong belief in a clear distinction between calculable risk and incalculable uncertainty. The economist Frank Knight is famous for an analytical distinction between risk and uncertainty that in many ways epitomizes these beliefs. Uncertainty, Knight argued, is incalculable while risk is calculable and hence knowable (Knight, 2006). Returning to the emancipatory ideals of modernity, we can say that the ideal was to turn as much uncertainty as possible into risk. The ideal was to objectify and control the future.

Risk in advanced modernity

Risk still serves to objectify a range of social, economic, technological and political problems. Probabilistic reasoning today is everywhere – in science, in finance, in insurance, in government. As we shall see later (above all in chapter 5), scientific (most often probabilistic) risks calculi are still ascribed more value than other conceptions of risk, and many political decisions are made based solely on such risk assessments.

Nevertheless, since the late 1960s the concept of risk, and its ensuing practices, have changed. According to Ewald, new ideas of precaution arose in the last decades of the twentieth century, and these to some extent have replaced the idea of solidarity and insurance (Ewald, 2002: 282). Solidarity and insurance have always had a third feature to them, namely prevention through scientific knowledge. But here a reversal has occurred. Side effects (that is, risks) of medical treatments, environmental problems and dangerous techno-logical products have undermined this belief in scientific knowledge. Rather than believing that all risks can be accu-rately known, assessed and managed, the conception is now that in many cases uncertainty remains and that some risks should therefore not be taken. The so-called precautionary principle is increasingly used (although often in more or less watered-down forms) in risk and health regulation. The pre-cautionary principle is based on the acknowledgement that new technologies often have side effects that are mired in uncertainty. The burden of (scientific) proof has shifted from danger to safety, so to speak: the responsibility is no longer to prove scientifically the danger of a given practice or tech-nology in order for it to be banned. Instead, if the safety of the practice or technology cannot be proven, the practice or technology should not be allowed (Timotijevic and Barnett, 2006; see also chapter 5). For Ewald, this new way of think-ing about risk is a historical milestone, because it means that calculable risk is no longer assumed to reduce incalculable uncertainty to insignificance. Instead, uncertainty is assumed to be of such importance that regulatory decisions need to take it into account.

Like Ewald, Ian Hacking focuses on the late 1960s as a turning point in the history of risk (Hacking, 2003: 27). Hacking points out an article by Chancey Starr in *Science* in 1969 on risk management. Risk management more than any-thing else epitomizes the belief that probability can reduce the uncertainty of the future to known risks and probabilities. However, Starr also acknowledges, first, that no technology is completely safe (zero risk) and, second, that there is no absolute threshold for when the risks of a technology should be accepted. Determining which level is safe enough is ulti-mately a political process; indeed, it may be said to rely more on values (and ethics) than on facts. Although science can inform us of the probability of things going wrong, science cannot decide how low the probability need be in order to be morally acceptable.

Both the idea of precaution due to uncertainty and the idea that there is no absolute given distinction between dangerous and safe undermine the idea of calculable risk. But, as Ewald also points out, risk is not the only idea that has been questioned in the last decades – so have the related ideas of social insurability and social solidarity. As has already been mentioned in chapter 1, a new and influential wave of neoliberal political thought has emerged that laments the loss of entrepreneurialism due to an excess of social insurance (O'Malley, 2004).

Conclusion

Risks are potential dangers, I wrote in chapter 1. The history of the concept of risk shows that with the advent of modernity risk came to mean *calculable* potential dangers. As such, risks came to signify the belief that humans could engage with and manage, if not the future, then at least potential dangers. The idea of calculable risk was hence an integral part of modernist ideals about shielding citizens from misfortune by means of rational forecasting, risk management of nature and technology, and social insurance. But with advanced or late modernity, these ideals have changed. Strong doubts, about both the human capability of managing risks and the desirability of doing so, have emerged. Above all, due to unintended side effects of technology, belief in the ability to calculate, to objectify, potential dangers as risks has somehow waned as has more generally the belief that humans can successfully plan and insure against future dangers. Knowledge of such side effects has, of course, also existed prior to late modernity, but in most cases the belief in technological progress tended to override these concerns (Andersen and Ott, 1988). Part of the current erosion of the belief in objective risk calculus is also the realization that potential dangers might be objectified, but what constitutes the acceptable level of *objective* risk is a *subjective* question. At the same time as the idea of objective risk is being challenged due to technological side effects, neoliberal political thought has questioned the economic and social benefits of social risk distribution. The desirability of collective forms of insurance has been questioned.

This is a crisis of risk, although not in the sense that there are fewer potential dangers. Rather, it is a crisis of the idea that these are calculable and manageable and that such calculation and management are beneficial. If one is to use Frank Knight's distinction between risk and uncertainty, then there is now more uncertainty and less risk. This uncertainty comes, to repeat, in two ways: fewer potential dangers are held to be calculable, and the desirability of risk over uncertainty has been challenged by neoliberalism. This crisis is a historical marker; it signifies a new stage of modernity. It is also the basis for the sociological interest in risk, because sociology studies the unintended side effects of technology, the values underpinning risk perceptions and the ideological renegotiations of the desirability of risks over uncertainty. The reader has probably noticed already that the three main sociological approaches to risk outlined in chapter 1 have reappeared here. The crisis of risk signals the beginning of a new sociological interest in risk.

This new stage in the history of risk is therefore the logical starting point for the chapters to come. But before moving on it is worthwhile to mention that this new stage does not mean that the idea of calculable risk has disappeared. Indeed, notions of calculable risk arguably thrive more than ever, as do the different expert professions that calculate and assess risks. This may seem a paradox, but it is nevertheless the case that all sorts of risk expertise are applied in all sectors of society at the same time that such practices and forms of knowledge are being questioned. An example, and perhaps also the clue to an explanation, could be the phenomenon of technology assessment. Since the 1970s technology assessment has been institutionalized in most Western countries in response to concerns about unintended side effects of technology. In other words, when faced with new uncertainties, most Western countries have responded with more risk assessments. Risk thus becomes an even more important concept when uncertainty emerges as a concern. Likewise, insurance has not been abandoned; rather it is changing and developing in response to the social and technological changes in society (Ericson and Doyle, 2004a; 2004b; Ericson, Doyle and Barry, 2003).

Another way of explaining this is to say that our perception of the future has changed. Modernity, I wrote at the start of this chapter, meant no longer letting the gods dictate the terms of the future. It meant a conception of the future that was more open, a future in which humans could engage rationally and strategically. With late modernity, this future is now becoming even more open and more unpredictable. Helga Nowotny, for example, talks of an 'extended present', arguing that the 'dramatic increase in complexity draws the future closer' (Nowotny, 1994: 52). One example of such complexity might be the unintended side effects of technology, but Nowotny and several others make the point that complexity not only enforces the idea that particular technologies are hard to control, but also the idea that the future itself is seen as unpredictable. The future becomes more present to our minds in a variety of ways. If there is a sense that the future is difficult to predict, more risk assessments might be deemed necessary. But so might precautionary measures. The same sense of the unpredictability of the future might also lead to neoliberal critiques of social insurance for reducing, say, the flexibility of the labour force, a flexibility that precisely is needed in an uncertain world.

The point is this: we shall now encounter some very different theoretical approaches to risk. Furthermore, descriptions of various sectors of society will show that while a sense of more uncertainty seems to exist, the idea of calculable risk does not go away; rather, it expands into new fields of application. But at least one thing does unite both the theoretical differences and the simultaneous, if not paradoxical, rise of both risk and uncertainty – it is a feeling in contemporary society that the future is unpredictable. By way of conclusion, we may say that society has turned Humean (Beck, 1992: 28). Risk and uncertainty means not knowing what to expect (Luhmann, 1993), and it means being aware that the causal relations between present and future events are complex and difficult to foresee. Faced with such an open future society is simultaneously becoming more sceptical about inductive prognoses for the future and increasingly forced to initiate and rely on such. Risk calculations therefore do not disappear but rather multiply. Moreover, such an open future poses dangers, but of course also possibilities (a theme to be explored in chapter 8). Risks and uncertainties are everywhere.

3
Theories about risk

Mary Douglas

Mary Douglas has developed what she calls a cultural theory of risk. She has evolved her ideas both alone and also together with several collaborators, including Aaron Wildawsky, with whom she wrote the book *Risk and Culture*. An anthropologist, Douglas has studied a range of tribal cultures. She draws on these studies when turning to contemporary Western culture and its notions of pollution and risk. Douglas is generally inspired by structuralism – that is, the idea that all cultures contain relatively fixed and stable systems of meanings and classifications. For example, any given culture has specific concepts of good versus bad or pure versus dirty, which are reproduced through narratives and rituals and other elements of culture. While what is concretely seen as pure or dirty is specific to a given culture, distinctions such as that between pure and dirty can be found in all cultures. The reason for talking about structure is therefore that the *elements* of the structure – what it is that is seen as pure or dirty – may vary across cultures, but all cultures have such distinctions that form a system of classification or a structure.

The classificatory systems described by Douglas uphold order in the world. They prescribe what the world consists of and what can be mixed and what must be kept distinct.

When this prescribed symbolic order is breached, people belonging to the particular culture perceive this breach as pollution. People in all cultures worry about the risk of pollution – that is, the confluence of things that should be kept apart. For example, Douglas asserts that the United States and other Western societies have become sensitive to pollution of the environment. As a contrasting example she mentions the Hima, a tribal people in Africa, who worry about mixing forms of food that must be kept separate.

Both of these worries are due to cultural cosmologies that stipulate a specific order that at times is threatened. Douglas often makes such comparisons between Western culture and other cultures. She does so to question the idea that Western ideas of risk and pollution are 'rational', making them distinct from 'superstitions'. Also Western contemporary ideas about risk and pollution, she argues, rest on values and culture (Douglas, 1984: 34–5).

Risk, in Douglas's view, is the threat of the classificatory system being thrown out of kilter. Such a breach is also a moral transgression. Moral values in turn uphold social and political order. For example, risks give a community a shared problem or enemy and can therefore be used to mobilize the community. Risks are, Douglas says, 'weapon[s] of mass coercion' (Douglas, 1992: 6). Dealing with risks always means finding out who is responsible, and here the moral and political order again rears its head. Douglas states that

> [I]n all places at all times the universe is moralized and politicized. Disasters that befoul the air and soil and poison the water are generally turned to political account: someone already unpopular is going to get blamed for it. (Douglas, 1992: 5)

For Douglas, the function of risk and pollution as vehicles for the maintenance of the social and political orders makes them comparable to taboos. A traditional community aspiring to cultural homogeneity uses sin or taboo to enforce this cultural integration. Those who are 'in sin' or 'under taboo' have violated the codes of the collective. The sense of community is thus reinforced and reproduced through a collective awareness of the dangers of sinning or breaking the taboo.

In distinction to taboo cultures, modern societies are less characterized by community and more by individuality. Therefore in modern societies the forensic use of risk (the blaming and causal attribution) is concerned with violations of (the right to) individuality. Alternatively, in the case of breaking a taboo, blaming has to do with violating the codes of the community. For the same reasons Douglas also thinks that the United States, which is more individualistic, is more risk-focused than are European countries.

Risk is not the same as sin or taboo, but Douglas argues that the differences are not due to taboos being after-the-fact reconstructions while risk is predictive, looking to the future. For people living in a taboo culture, taboo *is* a way of looking to the future (Douglas, 1992: 26). According to the Hima, their cattle will die if they eat agricultural produce together with milk. The Hima do not farm but a neighbouring tribe does. Cattle are the Hima's main economic resource and Hima culture stipulates complete separation from the neighbouring farming tribe. Hima risk culture serves to uphold this social order.

The most important point of Douglas's cultural theory is that perceptions of risk, including what makes for the gravest risks and who is to be blamed, are strongly biased by the classificatory and normative systems of a given culture (Douglas, 1982: 1). This should clarify why Douglas is seen as having a social constructivist's approach to risk. Certainly Douglas is a cultural relativist. She does not, however, want to dismiss risk as simply non-existent or unreal; indeed, she is highly critical of interpretations of her work that reach this conclusion (Douglas, 1992: 29). Instead, she argues that a cultural theory of risk heightens the awareness of the cultural bias of risk. Real risks do exist, but our perception of them is culturally biased.

Cultural values and modes of organization

Douglas notes that contemporary society has both lost faith in technology and become obsessed with probabilities (Douglas, 1992: 14–15). She is highly critical of the idea of objective risk, claiming that notions of objective probability exclude the subjective elements that are part and parcel of all risk perception. She is equally critical of psychological approaches to risk that, due to their methodological individualism, exclude the cultural factors; the self cannot be separated from the community, Douglas consistently argues. A central element in Douglas's theory concerns the cultural differences in risk assessment and the rise of sectarian values, which has led to an increased distrust of technology.

According to Douglas, 'culture is the publicly shared collection of principles and values used at any one time to justify behaviour' (Douglas, 1986: 67). We have already seen how Douglas relates these principles and values to social context. In her further analysis of different risk perceptions, Douglas draws on so-called grid-group analysis. Grid and group refer to two central characteristics of social membership, namely degree of autonomy (grid) and degree of incorporation (group). The matrix that Douglas constructs leads to four cultural categories. These four are cultural types, not personality types. The cultures are inextricably linked to modes of social organization and membership of social institutions because the cultures are products of organizations and social institutions and because they sustain these same organizations and social institutions (Schwarz and Thompson, 1990: 6).

In figure 1, grid and group are two continua, extending from a low degree of incorporation and hierarchical structure in the lower left-hand corner, and moving towards a very high degree of incorporation on the horizontal level and a high degree of hierarchical structure on the vertical continuum.

With this double matrix Douglas is able to describe central features of four different cultural types (in figure 1 each group occupies one of the four squares). Douglas applies grid-group analysis to different groups, modes of organization and social institutions. Various cultural groups within a social unit (for example a city) can be analysed, as can a society as a whole; or different societies can be compared. The fundamental assumption is simply that people belong to different social orders, some of which demarcate themselves strongly from the surrounding society and demand a high level of commitment from their members (high group) while others do not.

High structure

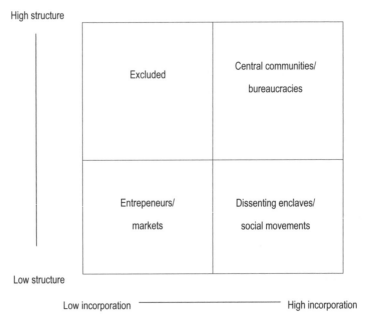

Low structure

Low incorporation ———————————————— High incorporation

Figure 1.   Douglas's grid-group model, adapted by the author from the matrix by Mary Douglas.

Some forms of social organization have very elaborate hierarchies and chains of command (high grid) while others do not. Culture varies accordingly.

Douglas, and her various collaborators, use different labels for the four types, probably because the labels can be applied to both groups, organizations and institutions. But if we lump together organizations and institutions, the categories can roughly be said to be the following:

1.   central or majority communities/bureaucracies;
2.   dissenting enclaves/social movements;
3.   individualists/markets; and
4.   the excluded (who suffer from lack of organization and subsequently have no political voice).

Starting in the upper right-hand corner we have high incorporation and a high degree of structure – that is, little individual autonomy. Douglas refers to this as the centre or the central community, the category comprising the organizations and institutions that are the heart of modern society. These organizations are elaborately structured and hierarchical, and thus conformity is relatively high. In the case of conflicts, there are institutionally embedded procedures for solving these. Much power is embedded in the centre and its bureaucracies, but the power is shared with the lower left-hand corner.

In the lower left-hand corner we have little structure and hence high autonomy and little incorporation. This space is occupied by individualists and entrepreneurs. As for social institutions, markets fit in here. The entrepreneurs are not only business entrepreneurs; any trendsetter or political leader, or anyone else working on the 'entrepreneurial edge of any profession or business' (Douglas, 1992: 118) is part of this group. The centre is dependent on this group, and Douglas asserts that an axis of power runs between these two poles. But the centre is also distrustful because any alliance with individualists is a fleeting one, as the individualists do not allow themselves to be incorporated into groups or subjected to hierarchies.

The lower right-hand space is occupied by the dissenting enclaves, which often form groups described by Douglas as sectarian (Douglas and Wildawsky, 1983). Here there is a high level of incorporation – the dissenting enclaves have enforced marked boundaries between themselves and others, and define themselves sharply against the central community. There is on the other hand much less structure and fewer formal rules, and consensus thus has to be established without the help of institutions and formal rules.

The upper left-hand position in the matrix is occupied by the excluded. They are under a high level of structural constraint – they are not excluded by choice – but there is a low degree of incorporation and they have very little voice.

To these four groups correspond different values, among them different attitudes to risk and environment. In one of Douglas's better-known analyses, she relates the different sets of values to specific perceptions of nature. She matches four of what she calls myths of nature to the four positions in the grid-group matrix (Douglas, 1992: 262). Douglas also asserts that differences in assessments of risks are tightly connected to different expectations about the future (Douglas and Wildawsky, 1983: 85), and she describes how the different groups perceive the future differently.

The centre, dominated by bureaucratic hierarchies, places much emphasis on proper procedures to address risks. For a member of the central community, it is hard to imagine that the stability of the hierarchies, the stable continuity, might ever be disturbed. If there are problems, the reaction tends to be regulation and control, perhaps sanction of those found to be liable, but always according to proper procedure. For the hierarchs, nature's ecosystem is robust, but only within limits. While radical disasters are generally inconceivable, too radical and sudden changes could tip the scales.

As has been mentioned above, there is an axis of power extending from the central community to the individualists, and they share also, to some degree, the way in which they perceive risks, because neither can imagine a radical catastrophe. But here the similarities stop. The individualists do not believe in time-consuming collective procedures but rather in quick decisions and personal responsibility; they assume that smart and fast personal decisions will solve problems, or rather, make them winners. For the entrepreneurial individualists risks are therefore problems, but they also constitute opportunities and promise rewards to winners. For the individualists, then, risks should be left to competing individuals (i.e. markets).

If we relate this to the future, the hierarchs believe in a continuation of the past into the future, with possible threats to continuity being dealt with in an orderly fashion by the hierarchical organizations; in contrast, the individualists see a much more open future where dangers, but above all rewards, loom. For the individualists, nature is robust.

The sectarians hold an opposing view: for them, nature is fragile. The sectarians worry about risk, and especially about pollution and damage to the environment. In *Risk and Culture* Douglas and her co-author, Wildawsky, devote considerable energy to describing the sectarian outlook because they believe that increased concern in the United States about pollution and environmental risk is due to the increased prominence of sectarian values in American society. Douglas and Wildawsky believe that most environmental organizations are sectarian. Calling environmental organizations sectarian can be puzzling because we tend to think of sects as religious, but this is not necessarily the case; 'sect' originates from 'a following'. Key to Douglas's understanding of sect is voluntariness. If we remain in the religious context, *churches* are something one is born into, while membership of a *sect* is something one chooses. As a result, sectarian organizations cannot rely on fixed authoritative procedures when faced with crises because the members might defect; the authority has little 'jurisdiction' (low grid). Sectarian organizations are often kept together by charismatic leaders, but consequently they may wither away without these. They are also prone to internal strife between factions. The sectarian mode of organization can be found only at the periphery; it is too unstable for the centre. Because of its marginalized position, the sectarian organization is free to criticize the values of the central community – indeed, it is in the organization's interest to do so. To keep members, a contrast between a corrupt centre and a pure periphery is often constructed rhetorically. With this come ideas about the purity of the sect and the equality of its members – and subsequently the threat posed to these from the outside. These threats often involve worldliness and conspiracy, which bring inequality and false beliefs, or the pollution of nature, which threatens purity. Hence sects imply a culture of fear, a fear of abstract doom, either religious or environmental, and this is precisely why environmentalism as an idea suits sectarian political movements. Risk holds appeal for the same reasons. In other words, sectarians build up strong boundaries between inside and outside, with the inside (themselves) being pure but threatened by the corrupt outside. For the sectarians the future itself is threatened.

The cultural typology Douglas has developed is used to analyse a cultural and political struggle, and because the excluded have little or no political voice they are given little attention. When it comes to the myths of nature, and to risk generally, the excluded are fatalists, viewing nature as capricious – the future has little good in store for them anyway. But in the struggle over what is most risky, the presence and importance of the excluded are negligible.

As has already been mentioned, Douglas and Wildawsky in *Risk and Culture* use the above analysis of sectarian culture to explain why environmental concerns emerged in the United States in the 1960s and 1970s. They argue that the United States had become more sectarian and that this, rather than the existence of genuine risks or environmental problems, was the reason for the concerns. It is hard not to read the description of sectarian values given above as slightly derogatory, and hard not to read *Risk and Culture* as cultural theory with a conservative political agenda. *Risk and Culture* is also problematic because it reduces political struggles over risk to a struggle between centre and periphery (Rayner, 1992: 91). The problems with this particular book should not, however, detract from the richness of Douglas's other work or from the analytical potential of grid-group analysis in general. Moving beyond the confines of grid-group analysis, Douglas's strong and important point is that risks are not objectively given facts but are as much about values. Even scientists, the standard-bearers of objective truth, are influenced by values. Discussions about risks therefore automatically become political. The weakness of Douglas's argument is of course whether or not all risks are reducible to culture, which she at times seems to imply. Yet at other times she also acknowledges that risks are horribly real, so one must conclude that Douglas should not be read as making strong constructionist claims.

Ulrich Beck

According to Ulrich Beck, risk has come to define the current stage of modernity. Beck begins his now classic book, *Risk Society*, by making a basic distinction between the industrial and the risk society, asserting that a transformation from the former to the latter began in the late 1960s. What defines the risk society, Beck argues, is a range of new risks – for example, environmental problems – which are unintended side effects of technological development. These new risks result from scientific and technological progress, which supposedly should solve, not create, problems. Beck makes a fundamental distinction between dangers and risks, defining dangers as caused by nature and risks as caused by humans. Risks are hence *manufactured* or *fabricated* uncertainties (Beck, 1992: 19). Social and technological development also caused environmental problems in industrial society; for example, inadequate sewerage or industry have also previously caused pollution and health risks. But, as distinct from these earlier side effects that were immediately noticeable, the new risks tend to be intangible, which means that they only can be known by means of scientific tests – and they are often latent, meaning that the extent of their damage only will manifest itself over time. Their latency is one reason why, even though they are to a degree knowable through science, the risks are not fully scientifically determinable. This means that the traditional technologies of risk assessment, management and insurance are no longer fully functional – the new risks Beck describes are in other words the uncertainties described in the final sections of chapter 2. Risks of the new type are often global or they traverse national boundaries; for example, pollution is rarely contained by national boundaries. Also it is often difficult to attribute responsibility, to pinpoint the causes of the risks and those responsible – Beck mentions a sign on an often jammed motorway outside his native Munich that says, you are not *in* the bottleneck, you *are* the bottleneck (Beck, 1997: 108). We are all responsible. Last but not least, many of the risks are on a catastrophic scale, meaning that they could potentially destroy human civilization. Humans are faced with their own potential to destroy social and technological development.

In *Risk Society* Beck claims that risks lead to political conflicts that are very different from the conflicts of the industrial society. During the industrial period the main social and political conflicts were over the distribution of wealth, while in the risk society the conflicts are over the distribution of risk (who is allowed to subject whom to which risks). The two conflicts are different, Beck argues, because they have different logics; the distribution of risk does not necessarily follow the structure of the distribution of wealth. 'Need is hierarchical, smog is democratic', Beck says in a much-quoted sentence (Beck, 1986: 48). However, he makes it very clear that, in many cases, the two distributions follow the same pattern, the only difference being that risks tend to sink to the bottom of the social structure while wealth rises to the top. Beck also states that new global inequalities emerge due to the global or transnational distribution of risk (Beck, 1986: 46). Beck's point is as much that risks become central to political struggles as that the logic of distribution differs from that of the distribution of wealth. Beck's argument that the distribution of risk differs from the distribution of wealth has drawn extensive criticism. As has just been described, Beck's argument is much more nuanced than the single statement that need is hierarchical but smog democratic, and he offers a keen understanding of global inequality and vulnerability to risks and dangers in particular (see also chapter 10).

There are other reasons why risk becomes contested. Indeed, the overarching theme of Beck's work is the uncertainty and uncontrollability that surround risks. The uncertainties often involve science. On the one hand, risks are made known to the general public through scientific research, but, on the other, science is also the original creator of the technologies that produce side effects and is therefore viewed with distrust by the public. Moreover, science and expertise often find themselves unable to unravel the complex side effects of equally complex technologies. Frequently there are conflicting research results about various forms of risk, which create ever new uncertainties, yet at the same time concerns about risk and criticism of science and technology are based on scientific knowledge and are voiced in a scientific language (Beck, 1986: 95). Environmental movements and other interest and lay groups also back up their arguments with scientific documentation. We are all exposed to science, all confronted with complex technologies and all bombarded with scientific information, says Beck. In the risk society, everyone has become a scientist (Beck, Giddens and Lash, 1994: 9). Or perhaps even more radically, the world itself has become a scientific experiment, in the sense that technology is being used in so many areas, with so many purposes, but without certainty that the intended purpose will be the only consequence. Therefore the use of technology is intensively monitored by scientists and risk regulators, much akin to the way in which they would monitor a scientific experiment in a laboratory.

Another reason for the disagreements about risks is that risks invoke values. Perceptions of risks differ, depending on political and moral values. Risks for Beck are real insofar as there truly are new technologies that have unintended side effects to an extent never seen before. But risks are also socially constructed because they are not so much disasters as anticipated disasters and because the very complexity of the technological side effects means that there is ample room for interpretations based on values. Risks are constantly defined, contested and interpreted in the public sphere, in political debates, in the mass media and so on. In these interpretations the 'objective' potential risks fuse with values, so that values defining what is right cannot be separated from facts about what is dangerous (Beck, 2007: 32). In regard to the latter point, Beck shares Douglas's thesis about the impact of cultural interpretation of risk, but he is also critical of Douglas because in his view Douglas *reduces* risk to culture only.

Initially, at least, Beck's main focus was on ecological risks (and also biographical risks; see below), but he has since dealt with other types of risk. He now roughly distinguishes three main forms of risk – namely ecological, financial and terror risks – without arguing that these necessarily make a comprehensive list or that the three categeries are mutually exclusive (Beck, 2007: 37). Throughout Beck's work a fourth type of risk – namely social, or what he calls biographical, risk – has also been analysed, but more in relation to his theory of individualization, a topic that I describe below. Terror differs from the other two types of risk because it is not unintended but rather very much intended. In many other respects, however, the risk of terror fits into the theoretical framework created by Beck; it receives much media and public attention, which places it on the political agenda and makes it subject to political conflicts about what should be done. Although intended, terror resembles the other risks in frequently involving technology – mobile phones were used to detonate bombs on trains in Madrid, and in the 11 September 2001 terrorist attack on the United States aircraft were used as bombs – and terror is of course very hard to control. Equally self-evident is that terror is increasingly becoming a global or transnational phenomenon, as are risks of the other types.

The risk of terror also fits with another element of the risk society – namely that the anticipation of terror, the fear of catastrophe, consumes much of our individual and our collective consciousness. In his later work (Beck, 2007), Beck draws a distinction between actual disaster and the potential for disaster, saying that many political struggles and culturally based perceptions concern merely possible or anticipated disasters. This also explains why we might talk of a risk society, even though death rates and other statistics show that life in Western societies generally seems safe. A risk society is oriented towards the future.

Reflexive modernization, individualization and cosmopolitanism

Beck's theory of risk is part and parcel of his larger theory of 'reflexive modernization' or 'second modernity'. We have already seen that Beck believes that a fundamental social transition has taken place (or is currently taking place) from an industrial to a risk society. A good deal of this change is due to the new risks and uncertainties that society is facing, which means that doubt and uncertainty are replacing trust and belief in progress through science and technology. Beck has used the notion of reflexivity to describe a modern society that increasingly is faced with the unintended consequences of its own progress. Therefore reflexivity does not mean that modern society or its members are more reflective about their actions. Rather it means that society is confronted with problems that are (unintentionally) self-inflicted.

Because reflexivity also connotes increased ability to reflect (and Beck's usage of the term is in fact not totally removed from this understanding), Beck has sought a different term for the historical development he believes to have taken place, namely *second modernity*. Beck's diagnosis is essentially one of a major crisis, and he has come to believe that 'reflexivity' does not capture this clearly enough. According to Beck the basic *institutions* of the modern industrial society, including family, state, work, science and so on, have been thrown into crisis because the major *principles* of modernity on which they rest – human rights, equality between the sexes, full employment, democracy, scientific rationality – have evolved to a stage where the basic principles and the basic institutions no longer correlate; global human rights undermine the political institutions of the national state, sexual equality puts the nuclear family under strain, the immense effectiveness of scientifically developed technologies creates side effects that science has difficulty controlling. This mis-fit is due to the *success* of the basic principles, to the complete saturation of the basic principles of modernity, and Beck is an outspoken defender of the basic principles, arguing for the need to transform institutions. For Beck, the current socio-historic epoch is not postmodern but rather radically modern – a period where modernization has succeeded to the degree that it becomes a problem to and for itself.

Besides risk, another important part of Beck's theory of reflexive modernization is his notion of individualization. With modernization, the individual is increasingly bereft of collective identity and belonging – for instance, belonging to a specific class. The individual is instead forced to construct her or his own biography, and to engage individually with the (changing) demands of various social institutions, such as work, family and politics. There is no doubt a high degree of freedom in this development, but there are also new pressures and pitfalls because individualization does not mean that, say, social inequality is diminished – it means only that the collective resources for dealing with social inequality are no longer there. This also indicates why the notion of individualization is in fact not that remote from risk, precisely because individualization leads to what Beck calls biographical risk. Pressures exist to make individual choices – for example, in careers – yet at the same time greater volatility in the labour market makes such choices risky. As has been indicated already, individualization does mean the freeing of the individual from the constraints of collective norms and institutions. But Beck, especially in later works, sees individualization less as people being freed to make their own choices and more as yet another unintended side effect of modernization. In particular, he points to how social institutions are founded on and promote ideas of individual rights, and hence he speaks of individualization as institutional individualization, as a social imperative.

During the last ten years Beck has been an outspoken advocate of cosmopolitanism, in no small part due to the conviction that global risks demand global or transnational political solutions and cooperation. For Beck, however, cosmopolitanism is not only a normative programme but also a challenge to existing methodologies and modes of thought in the social sciences. Beck has persistently criticized what he calls the methodological nationalism of the social sciences, that is, the most often implicit assumption that the given object of study is contained by national boundaries or, put differently, that the societies that the social sciences study are national societies. Social sciences, Beck argues, need a cosmopolitan approach, thinking beyond national boundaries, because most of the social phenomena under study today are transnational (I return to cosmopolitanism in chapter 8).

Beck is one of the most widely read social thinkers of today, and his status in, and influence on, the sociology of risk are undisputed. His theories have also been widely criticized. Beck has drawn criticism for focusing too much on risks as real phenomena rather than social constructs. This critique might apply to his first book, *Risk Society*, but in later works Beck has focused more on the cultural elements of risk and, as shown above, he certainly would not object to the statement that the cultural framework of the surrounding society influences risk perceptions. Several commentators have noted that Beck is in fact writing more about uncertainty than about risk or dangers. We saw the reasons above: for Beck, risks are incalculable. Therefore they would be defined as uncertainties if one were to maintain rigorously the analytical distinction between calculable risks and incalculable uncertainty. Beck readily acknowledges this.

Throughout his work Beck remains sympathetic to the project of modernity, and there is an optimistic belief in collective political action which can seem unfounded. Beck often comes up with examples where, using his term, subpolitical (see chapter 9) grass-roots organizations have exerted influence, but the question is whether these are battles won in a lost war. The commitment to modernity is no doubt the root cause of much of the criticism Beck has received. This commitment stands in opposition to postmodern and post-structuralist forms of social theory that believe neither in a grand theory of the type Beck believes in nor in social and ideological projects such as cosmopolitanism. Nevertheless, Beck's work on cosmopolitanism is currently generating a big following, and one might ask why new ideas and ideological programmes should have become obsolete and who, if not social scientists, should try to sketch out possible political solutions to society's problems.

Governmentality

Referring to a governmentality *theory* of risk is a bit of a misnomer. Foucault used the term 'governmentality' in the later stage of his career in an effort to reveal the changes in the nature of government that began in the mid-eighteenth century and unfolded in the following centuries with the emergence of the modern state (Foucault, 1991). Several of these ideas were subsequently developed into what now may be loosely referred to as a governmentality tradition by scholars such as Nikolas Rose, Peter Miller and Mitchell Dean (see Dean, 1999, for an introduction). A body of work on risk does exist that can be said to belong to this tradition, including the works of François Ewald, Nikolas Rose, Ian Hacking, Richard Erickson and Aaron Doyle, and Pat O'Malley. Nevertheless, this body of work is diverse, and lumping these scholars together in one category does not necessarily do them justice. In spite of this, for the sake of simplicity, I will in the following refer to a governmentality tradition or approach to risk.

The starting point for Foucault was the gradual emergence of a new mode of government that arose in the eighteenth century. Until then, rulers, feudal lords, kings or emperors had exerted control over areas that were of course populated, and with populations that needed to be controlled but not much more than that. In the eighteenth century, however, a new mode of government arose that saw as its task increasing the quality of life, the education, the health, the happiness and so on of the population. This was done through new forms of government, indeed through a new *science* of government, which relied not on physical coercion but on care giving and governance; and in these new forms of government power was increasingly dispersed and was embedded in new scientific practices rather than being centralized in a sovereign.

These new regimes relied much more on self-governing – that is, they impressed knowledge and beliefs on the population, which made it possible for individuals to take responsibility for themselves. Dean (1999) and others therefore famously talk of governmentality as a study of the conduct of conduct: modern power conducts the subjects into conducting themselves in certain ways. Much of this happens through education, knowledge and other 'technologies of government' (Rose, 1999: 52).

Knowledge and information about the population are crucial to responsible government. For that reason the new statistical technologies that became available in the nineteenth century have played a pivotal role in modern government. It is in fact only by means of statistics that the population can be monitored and hence rendered governable. Data on rates of birth and death, health and hygiene, education and skills, work, income, housing and families are the basis for governing. Such data simply construct, or objectify, the population as a governable object.

Not only statistics but also the concept of risk are crucial in this regard. In chapter 2 we saw that Ewald holds risk to have become one of the primary ways in which social problems become objectified and governable. According to the governmentality tradition, risk has become a central element in the 'assemblage of practices, techniques and rationalities concerned with how we govern' (Dean, 1999: 178). Governmentality scholars study in depth the usage of risk, along with other scientific and statistical concepts, because these types of knowledge have been crucial in constructing a governable population and in conducting the conduct of members of that population. Knowledge and thought are central in governmentality because such thought translates into government practices and knowledge is embodied in subjects, hence conducting their conduct. This also entails a strong focus on subjectivities. The modern state is a not a sovereign state exerting power by force. Indeed, Foucault holds power to be something exercised over people who could choose differently (Foucault, 1983: 221). The modern state creates individual subjects that are 'enabled' to govern themselves.

Knowledge and thought about risk do not stand alone, of course, and neither do statistical technologies. Rather, they are part of a multitude of sciences and professions, institutions and practices; schools, medical sciences, psychology, market research, asylums and prisons, among others, all play a part in the conduct of conduct. Yet, as we shall see later, it is crucial to recognize that risk as a concept is used increasingly in many of these disciplines and professions.

The governmentality tradition focuses strongly on (scientific) knowledge, including knowledge about risks, and how such knowledge helps to shape conduct. The approach taken to the study of such types of knowledge is relativistic. Governmentality scholars use historical studies – genealogies – of the development of scientific concepts and other forms of knowledge to show how they have changed over time and have been used in different ways to exert different types of power. For risks this entails a focus on how concepts of risk (and uncertainty) are used in different and historically changing ways and applied to different phenomena, in the process creating different governing mentalities. Much governmentality theory has had a keen eye on changes in the forms of government that have arisen in the last thirty or so years. For the governmentality tradition, these changes are related not so much to technological developments and environmental risks as to changes in risk management practices and managerial practices in general – changes that are linked to the rise of neoliberalism and the decrease of welfarism. The governmentality approach means studying concepts of risk and their usage rather than real risks or the perception of these.

Risks in current societies

Part of the interest in, and suspicion of, scientific bodies of knowledge concerns risk. Risk, and also uncertainty, have in different ways and at different times been conceptualized differently according to different governing mentalities. Governments have, at various times and in different ways, tried to shield the population against risks, to distribute risks throughout the population or to induce the population to take certain risks. We saw in the last chapter how Ewald has shown the central role played by risk in the emergence of welfarism. We have also briefly encountered O'Malley's study of how the relationship between risk and uncertainty has been redefined with the rise of neoliberalism. Another vital contribution of governmentality theory is that the distinction between uncertainty and risk is a fluid one that has been renegotiated over time and governmental practices may include both. In contradiction to Beck, who argues that there is more incalculable uncertainty today and less calculable risk, governmentality authors such as Rose, O'Malley and Dean use the distinction between uncertainty and risk as a purely analytical concept, focusing on how this distinction is constructed. O'Malley has focused in particular on how neoliberalism has advocated uncertainty and entrepreneurialism:

> The times demand that flexibility and love of change replace our long standing penchant for mass production and mass markets, based as it is upon a relatively stable environment now vanished . . . chaos and uncertainty will be market opportunities for the wise; capitalizing on fleeting market anomalies will be the successful business's greatest accomplishment . . . the strategy is paradoxical – meeting uncertainty by emphasizing a set of basics: world class quality and service, enhanced responsiveness through greatly increased flexibility, and continuous short cycle innovation. (Peter, 1987, cited in O'Malley, 2000)

As Nikolas Rose points out, this new valorization of uncertainty and entrepreneurial (and individual) risk taking was soon also voiced in what he calls a neo-social version:

> Look, we care about all our people and don't want anyone to suffer; we'll help the needy because we are concerned about them, but we must recognize the realities – we live in a global, competitive market; only countries with flexible labour markets will be able to succeed. You cannot rely upon the

state to provide you with unconditional security against risks and to protect you from the consequences of your own actions. (Rose, 1999: 145)

For O'Malley and Rose, such discourses represent a governing mentality wherein individual uncertainty is celebrated and social risk (or rather social insurance against such risks) discredited. However, this does not mean that risk as a concept (distinct from uncertainty) has lost significance. On the contrary, business, government and other social institutions now use risk technologies more than ever before. In finance, for instance, highly advanced probabilistic risk analysis and risk management play a more significant role than ever, while this industry at the same time epitomizes entrepreneurialism (see Bernstein, 1992; 1996).

Finance is of interest, too, because financial speculation has been conceived differently over time. As we saw in the previous chapter, various forms of insurance and finance were considered in medieval Europe to be usury. Later, governments banned various forms of finance because they were considered to be gambling. Insurance practices have also been banned for the same reason. O'Malley argues that it was at the end of the nineteenth century that the distinctions between financial speculation, gambling and insurance were governmentally invented (O'Malley, 2003; 2004: ch. 5). Of course, the process of distinguishing speculation from gambling has been ongoing since then (with the clear interest of legitimizing speculation by showing how it is not gambling). This applies, for example, to futures trading and trading in other forms of derivatives – practices that would earlier have been seen as gambling (which they indeed still are to some extent in some countries: Leslie and Wyatt, 1992: 88). With new probabilistic technologies, it was possible to create new products that could be traded in profitable markets. At the same time, the scientific models could be used to show that such forms of market trading were not reckless gambling. Again we see how the distinctions between risk (science and probability) and uncertainty (gambling) have been used and reworked.

Gambling itself has also become accentuated, if not valorized, in contemporary culture alongside a range of other cultural practices that involve risk taking (see chapter 8).

These practices range from day trading to mountaineering and other extreme sports. What unites them is not only risk taking (or in many cases simply submitting oneself to chance) but also their status as highly individualistic activities and as practices that seem to be surrounded by an ethos of personal 'deliverance', of overcoming dangers, of being a determined risk taker. This glorification of individual risk taking is arguably linked to the neoliberal trend of glorifying entrepreneurial individual risk taking (really: uncertainty taking).

Such changing scientific and political discourse shows two things. First, these governmentalities often take moral forms (Rose, 1999: 26). Today it is morally acceptable, indeed laudable, to be a risk taker. Second, such discourses are of course cultural in a broad sense – they relate to the prevailing values of a given cultural epoch. This connection between risk and moral values and culture represents common ground between Douglas's work and that of the governmentality tradition. But only up to a point. In Douglas's work, risks are mainly potential dangers external to society (e.g., risk of floods) or social constructions of such; in contrast, in the governmentality tradition risks are conceptualizations, ways of creating the social as a field for government intervention, and risks are hence internal (e.g., risk of unemployment). Moreover, while for Douglas the constructions and perceptions of risk create and reproduce an underlying social and political structure, governmentality theorists see these concepts differently. For them, these concepts are not signs or causes of underlying power structures but are powers (or part of power assemblages) in and of themselves.

The changes related to neoliberalism just described really concern uncertainty rather than risk. However, the governmentality tradition also identifies significant changes in the use of risk which have occurred in the same period. O'Malley (1998a) has studied extensively how criminology and various forms of crime prevention have adopted actuarial techniques. This development is part of an increased focus on crime prevention or, we might say, an increased focus on risk. The focus is on zones and environments where the risk (probability) of crime is higher, based on an implicit assumption that if the possibility is there, criminal acts will be conducted (see chapter 9 for more on this). In many ways a development such as this exemplifies a general government development that Nikolas Rose has referred to as the 'death of the social' (Rose, 1996). The idea of social causes, which emerged with social liberalism, as we saw in chapter 2, is to a large extent set aside (in later works Rose has argued for a somewhat similar 'flattening' of psychological thought, where psychological pathologies are reduced to malfunctioning chemical processes in the brain rather than being rooted in such things as upbringing).

Not only the export of actuarial techniques to various branches of government but also insurance itself has been extensively studied by governmentality scholars such as Ericson and Doyle (2004a; 2004b; Ericson, Doyle and Barry, 2003). Ericson et al. begin by specifying that next to the state, insurance is the most important institution of governance in modern society (Ericson, Doyle and Barry, 2003: 14). This is especially true of contemporary society, since the downscaling of the welfare state has led to more private insurance. Private insurance is not, however, a secluded business sphere. Insurance companies actively cooperate with the state in terms of legal frameworks, policing, surveillance and various forms of expertise. It is in this context that insurance as a method of governance and risk as a governmentality must be understood.

One of the ways in which insurance becomes a method of governance concerns the moral element of insurance (Ericson and Doyle, 2003). The extensive actuarial data amassed by insurance companies provide knowledge about 'normal' risk and 'normal' human behaviour. Human behaviour that falls outside the normal distribution, literally speaking, hence comes to be seen as not only abnormal but also by extension amoral. Insurance companies also seek to influence the insured; for example, health insurers will typically provide their customers with information on nutrition, exercise and so on. And, perhaps more significantly, insurance companies develop increasingly fine-grained systems for the risk profiling of customers, with resulting differences in premiums that provide customers with strong incentives to avoid risky behaviour (Ericson and Doyle, 2004b). This means, of course, that some people 'at high risk' are denied insurance altogether. Insurance also potentially affects the behaviour of the insured. For that reason, insurers try to avoid so-called moral hazards. An example is that there never really has been a market in private unemployment insurance. The worry is that this would create incentives not to work (Baker, 2003: 271–2). Of course a range of techniques are being used in various types of insurance to make certain that the insured conduct themselves responsibly without harming the collective.

The governmentality tradition has made crucial contributions to the sociological understanding of risk in the last decade. Governmentality theory does not focus on ecological risks but instead looks at the roles risk plays in the governance of modern subjects. One might object to the governmentality approach for precisely this reason, for wholly ignoring how the proliferation of technology has radically changed society. However, different theories have different applications, and we should simply accept that governmentality has little use in this particular (although undeniably crucially important) area.

One of the crucial contributions has been the analysis of the fluid distinction between uncertainty and risk, fluid both in the sense that it has changed historically and in the sense that it is discursively and rhetorically constructed. Since governmentality theories of risk constitute a diverse field of research, it may not be fair to point out that the relations between, and the totality of, the various developments of the advanced liberal society sometimes seem to escape the theories. I mention it nevertheless because diversity is not the sole reason. Another is the very theoretical style of the governmentality tradition, which avoids grand theoretical statements about epochal changes in society. The focus is always on the particular and the empirical. This does have merits. The social world changes more often, and in more diverse ways, than grand theories – for example, those about reflexive modernization – are able to convey. But, on the other hand, this style of theory also raises questions about whether or not links exist, say, between the use of risk in the criminal justice system and the neoliberal celebration of entrepreneurial uncertainty, or between the latter and extreme sports. Maybe there are no links, yet when it comes to risk we can observe more or less simultaneous changes in diverse strands of society. Is there a totality to these simultaneous changes that can and should be theorized as such? As Rose acknowledges, there can be 'strategic coherence' between a multiplicity of 'governmental techniques' (Rose, 2000: 323).

Other theories

The three theories presented above are arguably the three dominant theories of risk – at least in the Anglo-American world. A few other theories also deserve mention, however. Especially in his homeland but also in other parts of continental Europe, Asia and South America, the German sociologist Niklas Luhmann has enjoyed widespread popularity. Luhmann's theory is a highly abstract system theory, in which risk plays a significant role (Luhmann, 1993; 1995; 1998). Luhmann describes society as a communicative system that operates much like human consciousness: in society (a social system) there is a constant flow of communication, while in a conscious (or cognitive) system there is a constant flow of thoughts. Both communication and cognition are always about something; hence Luhmann says that both systems observe something.

Communication and thinking are similar because both are processes. They process information by creating meaning, that is, by conceptually ordering the world. Such a conceptual ordering is a complexity reduction, and it entails (i) selections and (ii) the formation of expectations. Regarding selections, no system can observe everything in the world; each has to focus on parts and often adopt only partial views of that which is observed. Regarding expectations, by imposing conceptual labels on things we communicate or think about, we also draw upon, and reproduce, expectations about the world. For instance, when we walk into a lecture hall, recognize objects in the room as chairs and sit down on them, we have used a concept, 'chair', and a reserve of knowledge about chairs, which includes the expectation that a chair will carry our weight. By using such expectations we need not pay constant attention to the object we sit on. We expect the chair to hold us, and we can shift our attention elsewhere, in this case to the lecture. We have 'gained time' – reduced complexity by narrowing our frame of expectations (see chapter 1), and can therefore concentrate on learning something new. In fact, expectations are just deselections of possibilities.

This example involves cognition, but Luhmann's point is that communicative systems are also forced to reduce complexity both by 'deselecting' and by forming expectations. But paying unequal attention to lurking dangers and narrowing frames of expectations are risky. And they turn on agency or, as Luhmann says, *decisions*. Any course of action might prove to be the wrong one. Based on this, Luhmann makes a distinction between danger and risk. Dangers are random events while risks are attributable to decisions, to individuals or society having actively (de-)selected and narrowed frames of expectations. Any complexity reduction (i.e., a decision) is risky, but in today's highly complex societies there is even more risk – that is, more pressure to make decisions. Societies often cannot afford to deselect anything, as so many things can turn out to be dangerous. When dealing not with simple objects or technologies such as chairs but with much more complex entities, societies may find that stable expectations are eroded, making deselections much more difficult. A risk society is a society that really does not know what to expect any more, yet is forced to make decisions.

The notion of risk is also central to Anthony Giddens's account of high modernity, arguably the most read and influential social theory of today. Like Beck, with whom Giddens's work on modernity and risks has a strong affinity, Giddens argues that society has reached a new stage of modernity. While modernity has reduced risk in some areas, high modernity also produces high-consequence risks that were not seen earlier – what Giddens calls manufactured uncertainties. In addition to ecological risks, Giddens mentions warfare, the rise of totalitarian states and economic and financial collapses (Giddens, 1991: 4). Once again, Giddens resembles Beck in emphasizing that these high-consequence risks are global in nature. The notion of trust plays a significant role in Giddens's work (Giddens, 1990), and of course also features prominently in regard to risk. Faced with a range of uncertainties involving the possible risks of technologies, humans are increasingly forced to trust experts, as the technologies (and their risks) are incomprehensible to the layperson. But in contemporary society expertise is also contested, Giddens claims – there are multiple authorities, which means that the decision on which expert to trust has itself become a risky one. For Giddens, this state of affairs is linked to reflexivity and individualization. In high modernity, people have 'no choice but to choose how to be and how to act' (Beck, Giddens and Lash, 1994: 75). This opening up of social life to decision making, which Giddens understands as a de-traditionalization, is linked to what he calls institutional reflexivity (Beck, Giddens and Lash, 1994: 185).

In chapter 8 of this book we shall be dealing quite extensively with voluntary risk taking and so-called edge work, that is, forms of activity that due to their riskiness and general breaching of social norms are on the edge of normality. The idea of edgework was introduced by Stephen Lyng (Lyng, 1990), and a theoretical approach is evolving around this notion, although the contributions are relatively heterogeneous. Lyng himself has, as we shall see in chapter 8, changed his definition of edgework quite radically since his first publications.

The last theory worth mentioning is the so-called actor network theory (ANT) developed by Bruno Latour, Michel Callon and others. Latour writes relatively little on risk per se, but the very starting point of his theory is the prevalence of complex technologies in modern society. Through these technologies, humans, as well as society, have become entangled with objects and nature to the degree that little is left of pure nature, society, subjectivity or objectivity. Instead, we have what Latour calls hybrids, or associations – complex configurations of mind and matter, nature and culture. Such complex configurations may also be risky. The technological hybrids may 'act' in ways in which they were not supposed to act, that is 'interact' with other things, setting in motion unintended causal processes. Things (technologies) sometimes strike back at humans (Latour, 2000). Latour's collaborator Callon has focused more specifically on how these hybrids, or 'translations' as they are called, very often develop in ways unforeseen and uncontrollable. I discuss this at length in chapter 4.

Finally, what was referred to in chapter 1 as psychometric research focusing on the psychological factors that impact on risk perception has been integrated into a multidisciplinary framework often referred to as the social amplification of risk framework (SARF). As the prefix 'social' shows, the focus has come to be not on the psychological factors but on how they interact with, are being affected by, and themselves affect, cultural and social factors. The SARF assumes that social perceptions of risk are social communicative processes, each involving actors and institutions (e.g. mass media) which are senders and receivers of information. At each transmission and reception both culture and psychological mechanisms as well as social and institutional dynamics factor in. As a result, the perceived gravity of a given risk can be either amplified or de-amplified. As written in chapter 1, one psychological mechanism might be the dread factor related to the fact that some technologies have low probability but high consequence risks. But a range of other factors affect the communicative processes. It might be easier for the mass media to create attention about some risks because they may be easier to represent visually – in pictures, graphic models or the like. The mass media are generally much better equipped for dealing with potential large-scale dangers than smaller, more mundane ones. Some risks might be ignored or suppressed if they run counter to culturally ingrained values. Through such processes, public perceptions of risks are formed. This is dealt with in detail in chapter 6.

Summary

This long review of social theories of risk shows a remarkable diversity. While Douglas focuses almost exclusively on environmental risks, Beck starts from the same point but broadens his outlook to include also uncertainties relating to the changing role of the welfare state and globalization. These last issues in turn form one of the starting points for governmentality studies, where the focus is on how concepts of risk render society governable. In choosing this emphasis, governmentality studies by and large ignore technology and environment. Douglas can be said to be taking a social constructivist approach; perceptions of risk hinge on culture and values. The degree of constructivism in governmentality studies is arguably even stronger, in that the focus is almost exclusively on conceptualizations of risks (Strydom, 2002: 47). In contrast, Beck's approach might be called weak social constructivism (Loon, 2002: 63).

Congruence is impossible, but the theories are never diametrically opposed either. Governmentality theories see risk not as real problems but as concepts which construct problems and corresponding technologies of government. Douglas's theory shares with governmentality theories a notion of constructionism, but here the focal point is cultural relativism. The same relativism, but in a softer version, is found in Beck's work. Beck in turn shares with governmentality theories a focus on individualization and neoliberalism, and the link between these and risk. This also appears in Douglas's work, but only to a minor degree and mainly as a way of explaining different perceptions of risk. Difference in perceptions is a theme which also appears in Beck's work, but not nearly to the same degree, while this theme is virtually absent in governmentality theory. Debates have raged among the theorists, especially between Beck and governmentality theorists. It is worth noting that when Beck talks of risk, he refers to what for governmentality theorists is uncertainty. And, as has just been written, risk for governmentality theories is above all a concept which creates certain realities and certain modes of government, while risk for Beck is a social problem. This is of course a fundamental difference.

While Beck and the governmentality theorists disagree on many issues, there also are many points of agreement. Both agree that new uncertainties have emerged and that the concept of risk is all-pervasive in contemporary society, and that it has fundamentally reshaped ideas about individual responsibility. Indeed, all three theories agree that a radical change has taken place since the late 1960s, although they draw radically different conclusions from it. All theories, furthermore, have a strong focus on knowledge (and uncertainty), but again in different ways. For Beck, knowledge and science are in crisis, whereas for Douglas science and knowledge are coloured by culture and always have been. For governmentality theorists, science and knowledge are core components in technologies of government. And, finally, all the theorists agree that risk is socially constructed at least to some degree, that risk relates to human actions and decisions and that risk moulds society. We will encounter the different theoretical approaches – hopefully in all their variety – in the following chapters.

4
Risk, technology and nature

Technology and being green

Nuclear power plants have probably been the most contested and frowned-upon sources of energy in modern times. The Three Mile Island accident in 1979 and the Chernobyl disaster in 1986 have consolidated public resentment towards this technology. The risk of accidents at power plants might be small, but the consequences are grave. And problems of storing slowly degrading radioactive waste only add to the feeling that this technology simply is too dangerous. The disaster at Chernobyl coincided with the publication of Beck's *Risk Society*, and that frightening disaster perhaps epitomizes a reflexive society that is deeply ambivalent about its own technological progress. However, other risks that threaten have created the possibility of a comeback for nuclear energy (although they certainly have not removed the ambivalence). The British government, for example, has revised its energy policy, which now includes the building of new nuclear plants together with accessing more renewable energy. The aim is to combat global warming. Somewhat ironically, given that opposition to nuclear energy was central to the formation of green movements, nuclear energy is now enlisted in an attempt to save the environment. Not surprisingly, opinions regarding nuclear energy remain divided, with environmental organizations reacting strongly to plans for more nuclear energy.

Nuclear energy is far from the only case of environmental groups reacting against energy policies that aim to reduce carbon dioxide (CO_2) emissions. Another example would be frequently occurring objections to wind farms. Often, such objections can be categorized as what has been called NIMBY (not in my back yard) objections. People simply do not want their views or immediate environment spoiled by a wind farm. Very often in these conflicts a discourse of environmental destruction is being used. Wind turbines are described as destroying nature. In several cases, such as the dispute over the Altamont Pass Wind Farm in California, environmental groups also have protested against wind energy. In the case of Altamont, the worry was above all the damage to raptor populations, but in other cases the worry has been the destruction of unspoilt landscape. When protesting, environmental organizations tend to emphasize that they support alternative energy, but that the proposed location is wrong or that other factors are ignored (in the Altamont case one argument is that at least the existing wind turbines should be replaced by taller ones in order to avoid the raptors' flight paths, something which is being done).

Such political conflicts help to show the role of nature in the risk society. First of all, they show that use of technology and the effects of technology are fiercely debated. Second, they show that notions such as 'nature' or 'green' or 'environmental' are ambiguous, subject to change and often used differently. Very different ideas about the preservation of nature can hence be found in such debates. What kind of nature is most important: birds, beautiful landscapes or the atmosphere? Is 'nature' or 'the environment' something pristine, fragile and untouched that must be protected from humans, or is it something that always has interacted with humans, that has always (or already) been changed by as well as changed human society? Is it something aesthetic or not? Is it at all visible? Third, and perhaps above all, such conflicts show one deciding aspect of the risk society, namely that in the risk society it is not only nature that is in danger, it is also human existence. Hence technological development no longer only negatively affects nature, it affects *us*, humans, as well. This creates a necessity to rethink precisely what nature is and how human society is connected to and dependent upon nature.

This chapter is mainly concerned with technological–ecological risks, that is, risks to the environment and/or to human health (as we shall see, distinguishing between these is often problematic) due to the use of technology. Technology can be many things; the term indeed refers to all sorts of tools that humans use to make their lives easier. Technology is often used to instigate and control specific causal processes; an electric kettle is used to cause water to boil, to offer a mundane example. It is easy to see that the number and scale of human technologies have multiplied with modernity. At least in the developed world humans have benefited greatly, but technology and technological production also bring problems. Technologies (such as nuclear fission) can first of all be potentially disastrous. Strict regimes of risk management are necessary in order to avoid catastrophes, the probability of which are very small but that would have grave consequences were they to occur. Second, industrial production has meant intensive consumption of natural resources and energy and, at the other end of the production process, large amounts of waste. And, third, industrial production – that is, the rational (in Weber's sense) ordering of production processes by means of technology, itself produces risk, not because of depletion of natural resources or because of the production of waste but because such production might trigger unforeseen causal processes. As an example, the BSE (bovine spongiform encephalopathy, or mad cow disease) crisis in Britain resulted from highly rationalized forms of production. Instead of grazing, cattle were being fed high-protein fodder pellets, produced in part from cow carcasses; for this reason, the disease spread very quickly. In cases such as these, elaborately designed production processes that are supposed to be *effective* turn out to have side *effects*.

Technologies, in summation, interfere with the environment and have the potential to backfire on a catastrophic scale. What unites these slightly different forms of risk is the causal power of complex modern technologies. This means that technology and industrial production are 'causally hooked up' with the natural environment. They drain energy from, feed back waste into and in various ways affect the natural environment.

Both unpredictable side effects and the depletion of natural resources are huge problems that humankind has to contend with. These effects and the potency of human technology in general are of such magnitude that little, if any, true nature remains. Global warming affects even the remotest places, such as the south and north poles. Today, most of nature has become cultivated land, and land that is not cultivated is often intentionally left alone (in many cases protected as nature reserves), increasingly enjoyed by humans for leisure activities such as hiking, mountaineering, wildlife photography and the like. In other words, the nature that has not been destroyed has become an object of consumption and leisure. Either way, nature today is subject to human control to an extent never seen before.

Technology and complexity

Charles Perrow has in a famous book amply demonstrated the fragility of complex technological systems (Perrow, 1984). By 'complex', Perrow means that such systems comprise what he calls tightly coupled elements, meaning that one given element in the system is related to, and can negatively affect, a range of other elements in the system. As a result, once something goes wrong, this very quickly, and irreversibly, triggers other parts of the system to malfunction also. Hence small mishaps can create big accidents, as was the case with Three Mile Island. Systems such as nuclear plants often comprise a range of safety features that reduce complexity by 'blocking' couplings between elements of the system (for instance turning off the nuclear reactor in case of malfunctions in the periphery of the system). But technological facilities may also have organizational structures and decision-making routines that counterbalance that. In the case of Three Mile Island, parts of the automatic safety system worked but others did not. Technicians, however, assumed that all parts of the safety system worked. These misconceptions and resulting actions ultimately coupled events into a process that led to the serious incident.

Perrow's conclusion is that accidents in complex technological systems are inevitable, or 'normal'. For that reason
Perrow recommends that nuclear technology be abandoned,
as the magnitude of a normal accident with that technology
is too immense. Much of Perrow's analytical approach is
systems-theoretic, which is also the approach of much risk
analysis (and the theoretical tradition from where the notion
of complexity originates). Perrow and his collaborators have
therefore been able to engage in a productive debate with
engineers and risk analysts regarding, among other things,
whether adding redundant safety features to a system (for
instance, a whole series of mutually independent sensors in
a nuclear plant) actually reduces risk (Sagan, 2004). The
systems-theoretic concepts of complexity and the related
terms 'non-linearity' and 'chaos' are increasingly used in sociology (Eve, Hornsfall and Lee, 1997; Luhmann, 1995) and
many other scientific disciplines (Prigogine, 1980; 1997;
Prigogine and Stengers, 1984; Waldrop, 1994). Complex
systems, whether the ecosystem, a pile of sand or a nuclear
reactor, contain elements that might affect each other in
unpredictable ways; this means that small initial changes
might produce big consequences or vice versa. Complex
systems are therefore often hard to predict and may behave
and evolve in unforeseeable ways. Complex systems can be
very resilient, but they can also at other times be very vulnerable to small changes.

Catastrophic side effects might have a low probability, but
social scientists have pointed out that such probabilities refer
only to the technological system per se. In real life, however,
the risk of a given technology also depends on the social
organization of which it is part. Indeed, a good part of the
unpredictability of technological systems is that they are
operated by humans and embedded in social organizations
and social environments (e.g. Wynne, 1996: 58). Sociologists
have shown how social conventions and norms may confuse
or even override the prescribed safety procedures. Once it is
put to use, technology does not stay 'pure', something that
risk analysts tend to forget.

With increased technological complexity, the ways in
which technology interacts with the environment become

less tangible, visible and 'smellable'. This is one of Beck's starting points for his risk society thesis (Beck, 1992): we cannot see, hear, smell or feel, say, carcinogens in our food or carbon dioxide being emitted into the atmosphere. But not only are such risks intangible, they are also latent, in that the negative side effects may only manifest themselves many years after the risk was 'produced'. And, lastly, they may spread over vast distances. Adam elaborates on this by using the German terms *Merkwelt* and *Wirkwelt* (Adam, 1998: 24–35). *Merkwelt* is the tangible world, while *Wirkwelt* is caused by human action and is indeed a world of hidden cause and effects. Adam's point is that these two worlds are drifting further and further apart in the risk society, especially in regard to time. The *Wirkwelt* is latent but it may manifest itself as a tangible *Merkwelt* sometime in the future. The effects of carbon dioxide emissions, for instance, for a long time belonged to the *Wirkwelt* and are only now slowly starting to manifest themselves as tangible changes in global weather patterns.

Nature, environment, ecology

Riley Dunlap notes that when risks and pollution become invisible, are no longer local, and have long-term effects, the perception of nature and pollution also changes (Dunlap, 1997: 27). Nature ceases to be conceived aesthetically – as, for instance, a vision of untouched land with blue skies, green grass and clear water – and pollution ceases to be the opposite of such aesthetic nature – for instance, in the form of scorched land or muddy rivers. Instead, pollution becomes something related to human health. Dunlap's remarks indicate some of the intricacies of the concept of nature. The aesthetic understanding of nature as unspoiled, idyllic landscape is an understanding of nature as something 'out there' – that is, separate from human culture and society. The other understanding, created by the awareness of invisible risks that threaten human well-being, is an understanding of nature 'in here' – that is, an understanding of nature as something of which humans are a part and on which they depend. Nature 'in here' is something that cannot be destroyed or harmed without ourselves being harmed.

The distinction between nature 'in here' and 'out there' has – in various guises – been subject to extended analysis and discussion in recent years (Beck, 2000; McLaughlin, 1993; Macnaghten and Urry, 1997; Murphy, 1997; Rogers, 1994; Rosa and Dietz, 1998; Strydom, 2002). There are, however, different versions of nature 'out there' and 'in here'. Nature 'out there' might be perceived aesthetically as something pristine that must be kept so. But such nature 'out there' might also be seen as something dangerous that must be controlled. The human control of nature was (and is) a significant element of the ethos of modernity. A philosophical division between nature ('out there') and human society made such control feasible. We saw in chapter 2 how modernity brought with it a division between society and nature that gave impetus to the idea of social problems. Another consequence of this division is that it gave impetus to the human colonization and exploitation of nature – because in order to control or exploit something, one must be detached from it.

Ecological risks have created a new awareness that nature is not a separate sphere that humans can use and exploit without repercussions for society and human life. Risks show how society is entangled with, rather than distinct from, nature. If drinking water gets contaminated, or if weather patterns are affected by carbon dioxide emissions, or if wheat contains toxins, what is bad for nature also becomes bad for humans. Nature ceases to be 'out there', wholly separate from human society. This is a central element of Beck's notion of reflexivity and, as we shall see shortly, a similar notion is prevalent in Bruno Latour's work.

The distinction between nature 'in here' and 'out there' is in most cases to be found in analyses describing real existing changes in the relationship between nature and society. But as Douglas and others have shown, *perceptions* of nature are also important because they influence the perception of risk. What nature is – the nature of nature – is therefore ultimately a political question. No doubt the primary rift continues to be that between industrial and reflexive conceptions of nature, that is, between industrial use and environmental concerns about sustainability (Strydom, 2002: 125). But there are also other categories of nature. Clark and York distinguish between three main positions (Clark and York, 2005). The first sees nature as robust and exploitable; the second sees nature as a fragile ecological system, a so-called 'deep ecology'; and the third sees nature as something with which society has always interacted but on which society also depends.

Mary Douglas, we saw in chapter 3, identifies three different conceptions of nature, according to which the central community represents a middle-of-the-road approach between entrepreneurial ideas of nature as robust (corresponding to the first notion of nature) and sectarian ideas of nature as fragile (corresponding to the second). Whether Clark and York's third position matches that of Douglas's central community is more questionable. The reason why they might not be comparable is due to the fact that Douglas's typology is mainly concerned with how robust or fragile nature is rather than whether or not society is totally distinct from nature, or whether nature is viewed aesthetically or functionally.

Such incompatibilities show how multiple conceptions of nature abound, both in the social sciences and when it comes to scientific classifications of nature. Differences in conceptions of nature might seem marginal to the subject of risk. But they are important because risk changes our understanding of nature and because our understanding of nature influences our understanding and perception of risk.

Symbols of nature are very often invoked in debates about risks. Because nature, in whatever guise, has positive connotations to most people, it is a powerful symbol. For example, the polar bear has become an important symbol in the discussion about global warming because melting ice caps in the Arctic threaten it with extinction. Its role became pivotal when, towards the end of 2006, the US government put the polar bear on the list of threatened species, thereby officially recognizing for the first time, if only tacitly, the threat of global warming. It is worth noting that animals have become the impetus for political responses to a problem that just as easily could have been framed as a social or economic problem rather than a natural one. There is no doubt that symbols of pure and wild nature possess an emotional force that is often used to evoke environmental consciousness. It is easier to get a message across to the public using a straightforward symbolic figure such as the polar bear than to get one across about complex and invisible physical processes that might influence weather patterns over a span of thirty years. For this and many other reasons, slogans about nature, such as 'save the whale' or 'keep nature clean', abound. Such conceptions of nature are also easily represented visually, which is important in modern medialized society, and they create emotional resonances that nature 'in here' cannot. So even though Dunlap has argued that nature has attained a meaning with less emphasis on aesthetics, it is still symbolized as pristine, perhaps even sacred, wild surroundings untouched by humans.

Risks as hybrids

The two main themes dealt with until now – technological complexity and the loss of nature 'out there' – figure prominently in Bruno Latour's actor-network theory (ANT). Latour opens his main work, *We Have Never Been Modern*, with a list of some of the strange technological phenomena that are so plentiful in the modern world – the hole in the ozone layer, HIV-infected blood banks, rare flowers growing on slag heaps in rundown mining districts, whales wearing radio transmitters. The examples show how nature and culture have become more and more entangled, but note that (the first) two examples are also examples of risk. As we shall see, ecological risks are by definition hybrids of nature and culture.

Latour, like many others, argues that one key element of modernity was the separation of culture and nature. Latour refers to this cornerstone of modern thought as the Modern Constitution. The nature–culture divide has strongly influenced Western philosophy and science since the Enlightenment, and it has served as the impetus for amazing scientific and technological developments since then. The separation has been consequential or effective because it has formed the basis for modern science, which has created many new technologies of the kind mentioned above. But this 'success' has also put the Modern Constitution under strain. Technology creates ever more numerous connections between nature and culture, new complex technological configurations that transgress and break down the dichotomy of the Modern Constitution. By in effect connecting what it claims to separate, the Modern Constitution is undermining itself. Somewhat tongue in cheek, Latour contrasts the (now failing) nature–culture divide of the Modern Constitution with pre-modern cosmologies that stressed the interconnectedness of humans and nature. Faced with ever more technological connections between nature and culture, we are starting to realize, as Latour puts it, that we have never in fact been modern.

> Let us say that the moderns have been victims of their own success. It is a crude explanation I admit, yet it would appear that the scope of the mobilization of collectives had ended up multiplying hybrids to such an extent that the constitutional framework which both denies and permits their existence could no longer keep them in place. The Modern Constitution has collapsed under its own weight . . . (Latour, 1993: 49)

Latour is wary of notions such as late modernity. Instead, he claims that a return to non-modernity has happened. Nevertheless, he, just like Beck and other risk theorists encountered so far, conveys a sense that a radical change has occurred in recent years, a technological proliferation, an increase in complexity or what he intermittently calls a lengthening of the networks or an increased hybridization (Latour, 1993: 117). Latour's theory is, as has been said, not about risk per se, yet it contains a strong emphasis on new types of risk in that he emphasizes the causal complexity and interconnectedness of the world – complexities that lead to uncontrollability, nonlinearity and risk (Latour, 2000; 2003: 36; Law, 1999; Law and Mol, 2002).

Latour more than anyone else shows how such connections dissolve the boundary between nature and culture. Key to this is his notion of actor-network. For Latour, actor-networks are the relations created whenever humans engage with things or nature. By engaging with each other, humans, things and nature also affect and transform each other (Latour, 1999: 15) – they become hybrids. Technological development means longer and more complex actor-networks. Latour also calls such hybrid actor-networks 'translations' or 'associations'. One of the reasons for why he uses such terms is that the networks he refers to are not necessarily static but are, rather, processes. Going back to the BSE crisis, modern agriculture is a complex translation in the sense that it is a production process involving livestock, science (e.g. veterinary science), technology (fodder production), industrial production (fodder production, meat processing) and humans. The longer the translation the greater the risk – that is, the greater the risk that something, somewhere, in the production processes of the network might go awry. Similarities with notions of complexity and nonlinearity are clearly visible here.

Latour's close collaborator and 'co-founder' of ANT, Michel Callon, also conceives of things such as technological industries as specific configurations of translations or associations. Their specific configurations Callon refers to as *frames* (see, e.g., Callon, 1998: 16–17). Framing is a process whereby complex networks are disentangled, creating some sort of order. One example of such a framing (once again with reference to BSE) could be the elaborately designed configuration of modern agricultural production as mentioned above. That network, however, proved to be evolving in an unpredictable and uncontrollable way. It evolved outside the frame. Callon refers to such uncontrollable networks or translations as *hot translations*, and he speaks of such hot translations *overflowing* frames. Side effects, in this case the spread of mad cow disease, overflow frames. Callon also uses this concept in areas not related to technological–ecological risks, but he very often uses technological side effects or ecological problems as examples of frames being overflowed. Callon argues that new frames will then be constructed, but he does not expect any such frames to last. Socio-technological development always means more hot translations.

For Latour, actor-networks are never purely social, nor are they subjective, natural or objective; these analytical categories all lose their currency. All 'things' are hybrid, half object and half subject, continually crossing the boundaries between these categories. For example, innovation is not just about getting great ideas but about mobilizing new networks of both things and ideas (connecting things and ideas). Scientific ideas and discoveries are not just ideas, but the result of, and dependent upon, objects such as laboratory equipment. Latour's favourite example of this is the discovery of the vacuum. Without a glass pump, the vacuum could not have been demonstrated and made visible: ideas without objects do not matter much (Latour, 1990).

Having cast aside the distinction between culture and nature, Latour lays out a rather distinct notion of the natural environment in his work. One way of describing his notion of nature would be through his use of the term 'ecology'. Ecology, Latour argues, does not mean a closed sphere beyond the human or the social but precisely the opposite. Ecology is a complex network of all things human as well as non-human. Ecology is about interdependency – interdependency between humans and nature being one kind – thereby transcending any idea of nature as being distinct from culture. For this reason Latour is critical of (in his eyes, false) ecological thinking that advocates the 'improbable belief in the existence of a nature external to humans and threatened by the latter's domination and lack of respect' (Latour, 1998: 230–1). Latour, perhaps more than anyone else, epitomizes the third of the three previously described conceptions of nature. Latour writes that an ecological approach does 'not at all say that we should not use, control, serve, dominate, order, distribute or study them ['natural' entities], but that we should, as for humans, never consider them as simply means but always also as ends' (Latour, 1998: 228). Hence Latour advocates ecological politics, which, he says, 'has nothing to do with nature' (Latour, 2004: 5) and is critical of the other form of environmentalism, deep ecology, which sees nature as a fragile ecosystem in which humans should not interfere (Latour, 2004: 26). Latour laments this lurking rift in environmental politics because he fears that it weakens the political power of environmentalism; however, he also expresses the hope that actual environmental political action creates a new common ground which for him has to be based on an understanding of nature as something 'in here', deeply connected with human society.

Risks are potential dangers often surrounded by uncertainty and controversies. Risks are often ambiguous and invoke values and therefore attain a subjective quality. This fact has lead to much debate and a bulging literature on the social construction of risk (that is, the perception of risks based on cultural preferences). Latour is very critical of such notions of social constructivism because he finds that such accounts put much too much emphasis on the human perception of the material world and not enough emphasis on things in themselves (not to mention the processes whereby things and human subjectivity become entangled with each other). The next two chapters will deal with uncertainty and differences in risk perception, but, given Latour's misgivings about the notion of social constructivism, it is worth outlining here why technological complexity can create uncertainty and be perceived differently seen from an ANT perspective.

In actor-network theoretical terms, risks are the possibility of complex actor-networks evolving or acting in ways other than expected and intended (Loon, 2002). Such networks are translations or associations, to use Latour's favourite terms. 'Association' has two different meanings that are used by Latour in combination. Associations are both real groupings, as in a political association, and mental activities, relating one thing to another.

Risks are associations in both of these senses. For example, through science humans are able to associate carbon dioxide emissions with global warming and global warming with extreme weather. But these are at the same time real causal links, created by human science. The simple point of this is that even though they are only potential, and even though they can only be grasped through associations, risks have a material reality to them as well. Rosemary Robins illustrates this in a study of a conflict between a company seeking permission for the construction of a GM human insulin facility and a citizens' group protesting against the plant (Robins, 2002). In the hearings about the possible risks of producing GM human insulin, both parties came up with detailed descriptions of the technology. The citizens' group framed the issue more broadly than the company, emphasizing the inherent unpredictabilities and risks. A Teflon filter considered by the company to be a foolproof security device removing any risk of contamination presented cause for concern for the citizens' group; according to the latter, the pores were a fraction too big, which meant that if metal particles were accidentally present in the gases to be filtered, the filter might not be wholly efficient.

The merit of such ANT-inspired analyses is that they show how the multiplicity of risk perceptions is grounded in the ability of technology and human knowledge to associate – that is, to form ever new hybrids. While cultural theories such as Douglas's explain risk by culture, hence reducing risk to a social construction, here risk is, at least in part, real and material. Robins argues that the risks perceived by the citizens' group and by the company are equally real because both accounts are associations. Neither is more socially constructed than the other.

On the other hand, the weakness of ANT is the inability to explain *why* different groups associate differently. That difference is a difference in the framing of expectations. In the example just given, the company seeking permission created a simpler, much more ordered and disentangled account of how the system would work. On the other hand, the network that the citizens' group mobilized was more complex, with more unpredictable chains of causation. The pertinent question is, then, what shapes the differing expectation framings of these technological processes, leading to different perceptions of risk. This question will be taken up again in chapter 6.

Global risks, vulnerability and inequality

Latour reminds us that risks have a material side to them. Based on that, it is pertinent to ask how risks are distributed, socially and geographically, and whether technology can also be a material resource for managing risks. The social distribution of risk seems to a large extent to follow the distribution of wealth and other resources (Mol, 2003: 79–84). Nevertheless, the correlations between social inequality and vulnerability to risk have often been ignored (Kasperson and Kasperson, 2005: 25–6), even though there is a burgeoning field in public health studies that addresses the impact of risk on mortality and socio-economic status, and there is also a body of literature on environmental justice.

Such socially caused differences in the distribution of risk are often amplified as risks – global warming being a case in point – increasingly become global problems, hitting poorer regions of the world relatively harder than richer regions. Key to the differences is vulnerability. Vulnerability depends both on the exposure to possible dangers and on resilience and sensitivity to such dangers (Kasperson et al., 2005). All may be equally exposed to risks, but the means for adapting to and offsetting the risks varies, depending on the economic and technological means available. As a result, differences in *vulnerability* are not only due to differences in the exposure to risk but also to differences in access to insurance, health services, technology, science, infrastructure, and efficient government and regulation, all of which are things that are more likely to be abundant in the industrially developed world – often, as it happens, the parts of the world that are responsible for creating the risks in the first place. The less developed countries thus frequently find themselves in a double bind. They are exposed to risk that is not always of their own making without having the means to avoid it. This double bind is arguably an element of a larger problem that especially affects the African continent (Mol, 2003: 10). In spite of being cut off from the benefits of economic globalization, many developing countries still suffer the negative effects of economic development, one of which is environmental degradation. But the unequal distribution of risks does not stop there. Regulation is an important factor, one example of this being workplace safety measures that are often weak or poorly enforced in many poor countries, leaving workers unprotected against unhealthy work environs. Combined with the fact that much 'unclean' industrial production today takes place outside the Western industrial countries, this has devastating effects on many people, for instance the workers who are wrecking old ships on beaches in India, thereby exposing themselves to dangerous substances, or the workers in China's chemical industries, who experience even more dangerous working conditions.

These are global inequalities, but there is reason to assume that inequalities also exist nationally, although this area of study is relatively under-researched. Kasperson and Kasperson mention that it will be the poorer and older populations in mega-cities around the world who will be vulnerable to such things as heat waves (Kasperson et al., 2005). When Hurricane Katrina struck New Orleans, the poorest sector of the population suffered the most because they were less mobile and often uninsured. Similarly, unevenness of access to health care may increasingly be a source of immense inequality as medical technologies become more sophisticated but also more costly, with many countries already struggling to cover the cost burden imposed by an ageing population. To conclude, risks do not obliterate social inequalities but rather redistribute them in ways with which the institutions of first modernity, to use Beck's vocabulary, cannot cope.

Summary

I have suggested in this chapter that human society is connected to nature – and that the intensity of these connections has increased with the proliferation of technology. That increased intensity is also the source of risk. The causal processes, feedbacks and repercussions among technology, society and nature are what create many of the side effects and potential dangers of the risk society. In describing, comprehending and debating these risks, I have evoked various notions of nature and the natural. One may talk of a loss of nature in the sense that there is more technologically influenced, controlled or manipulated nature and less untouched nature. The result is that less is 'naturally caused'. Hence there are more risks and fewer dangers, because the scope of human responsibility is radically enhanced. 'Natural causes' disappear, as does random nature. Everything bears on humans.

The technological entanglement of society and nature seems unavoidable and irreversible. Increasingly, the risks attached to technologies can only be fixed through other technologies. Nuclear plants can be built to reduce global warming, and medical technologies can be mobilized against increasingly prevalent diseases, such as cancer (caused not only by affluent Western lifestyles but also by such things as ozone depletion and carcinogens). In other words, technology secures adaptation, making those who have access to technological means much less vulnerable than those who have not. Insurance – for example, health insurance – is one of several other crucial factors that decide who are vulnerable and who are not.

5

Risk, knowledge and uncertainty

As new contributions to knowledge bring about a new awareness of something else not yet known, the sum of manifest human ignorance increases along with the sum of manifest human knowledge.

Merton, 1987: 10

Yet risk society, in opposition to the image of the term, captures a world which is much more open and contingent than any classical concept of modern society suggests – and is so precisely because of and not in spite of the knowledge that we have accumulated about ourselves and about the material environment.

Beck, 1998: 11

Does science know?

It is only a small step from risk and technology to risk and science, and an even smaller step from risk and science to risk and uncertainty (for an overview see Yearly, 2005: ch. 9). Environmental and health risks are intrinsically related to science and knowledge – and to uncertainty. Global warming is but one example of how such risks only become knowable thanks to science – and of scientists debating just what it is we know. Many risks are surrounded by scientific controversies and scientific uncertainties. The risk of global warming has been on the scientific and public agenda since the mid-1970s, but mired in scientific controversy. Scientists have debated, first, whether global warming is really occurring at all; second, whether it is caused by human activity; and, third, what the extent of the harmful consequences will be. There is here, however, as in many other cases, a slow movement towards scientific consensus. The UN Intergovernmental Panel on Climate Change now asserts with 'high confidence' (Intergovernmental Panel on Climate Change, 2007: 4) that global warming is occurring and that it is caused by humans. Symptomatically, the report includes an appendix in which statements such as 'likely', 'very likely' and 'high confidence' are defined. This last means that there is a nine out of ten chance that the statement is true (Intergovernmental Panel on Climate Change, 2007: 21). But even though scientists seem to be getting nearer to consensus, the issue is still mired in controversy, although a political consensus now also seems to be forming.

Scientific uncertainty and the need for decisions on risks in spite of uncertainty affect not only political decision making but also people as individuals. To give an example, women approaching or experiencing the menopause often face a dilemma. Hormone replacement therapy (HRT) can ease many of the physical and psychological symptoms and discomfort that frequently accompany or are caused by the menopause. It also helps to prevent osteoporosis, and there is evidence that it decreases the risk of bowel cancer. HRT in other words dramatically improves quality of life for many people, but with HRT also comes a slight increase in the risk of diseases such as breast cancer, stroke and thrombosis. For that reason, experts today generally do not recommend long-term HRT, mainly used to prevent osteoporosis, but still recommend short-term treatment, used to lessen the discomforts of the menopause.

The decision as to whether or not to undergo HRT is to a large extent left to women to make individually. The expert medical position in most Western countries is that there are so many individual factors and so much uncertainty that it makes little sense to come up with anything more than broad guidelines. For instance, in the case of individuals with a genetic disposition to osteoporosis, long-term HRT might be beneficial, whereas for individuals with no such disposition, the risks of long-term HRT might outweigh the benefits. But the dividing line between cost and benefit is fuzzy and uncertainties abound. And in addition to the purely medical concerns are such factors as the risk of weight gain, which experts often deny exist but are common knowledge among laypeople (Green, 2002).

HRT provides a multifaceted illustration of the complexities of risk that burden many people. One such facet, relating to chapter 4 and therefore mentioned only briefly here, is how medical intervention in female menopause changes what used to be considered natural – a stage of life for all women – into something approaching an illness that can be fought with drugs. But with the power to intervene comes also the burden of decision. Another facet is the changing role of experts (here, doctors) and laypeople (here, patients). The decision process is a far cry from the traditional distribution of roles, in which the expert would act as the authoritative figure, giving orders to the submissive layperson. Now, the doctor is more likely to ask, 'What do you think?' Indeed, today such a doctor–patient relationship is institutionalized – for instance with managerial concepts such as 'a patient-centred NHS' in Britain. The role of experts has, in this case and many others, changed.

Although very different, global warming and HRT are examples of how problems and practices are increasingly organized around concepts of risk – which was key to the definition of the risk society in chapter 1. In both cases, moreover, scientific expertise features strongly, and people are exposed to scientific expertise and confronted with a need to make decisions. This chapter will deal extensively with the problems of scientific risk assessment and discuss how science becomes entangled with politics and public concerns.

Science in the risk society

The role of science when it comes to risk seems both problematic and paradoxical – and in more ways than one. First, without science no one would have any knowledge of a broad range of risks and the technologies causing risks would not have come into existence. Second, public concerns about risks are often accompanied by distrust of scientific assurances that the technologies are safe, and yet public concerns are in many cases based on scientific findings. Third, science seems to produce as much uncertainty as certainty. As the quotations from Merton and Beck at the beginning of the chapter show, science generates as many vague indicators of unknown possibilities (risks) as it generates positive certainties.

Many public and political discussions hinge on science. In these discussions, scientists often contradict each other, and they are challenged by laypeople, politicians and political activists, who legitimize their own arguments by simultaneously referring to scientific findings and voicing distrust of other scientific arguments. Increasingly interest groups have their own experts and conduct their own studies which add more science, but not more certainty, to the debates (Irwin, 1989). So many uncertainties are exposed that the idea of science as the bearer of positive knowledge is being seriously contested. Yet – and this adds one more paradox to the list above – whereas scientific uncertainties and controversies could lead one to assume that science as an institution is in deep crisis, science nevertheless continues to be *the* source of authoritative knowledge. Scientific knowledge is everywhere and modern people understand the world, others and themselves on the basis of scientific knowledge (Yearly, 2005: vii). Indeed, science's institutionalization and monopolization of authoritative truth seems to increase globally (Drori et al., 2003). There are many reasons why science has this privileged role, many of them unrelated to risk. But it is certainly also because the increased awareness of risk grants science importance.

Many risks are intangible (see last chapter) and they can be 'known' only by means of science (Eden, 1998). Rachel Carson's 1962 book *Silent Spring* is seen as a landmark in the history of modern environmentalism. Carson, a chemist, argued that the use of pesticides has a range of detrimental side effects. Her book was a landmark precisely because it represented one of the first times that science was used to identify risks, an identification that then became the basis for environmental political activism. As Hironaka has pointed out, modern environmentalism has come to rest on science, as it is only through science that possible side effects and dangers can be fathomed (Hironaka, 2003; see also Eden, 1998; and, with some important qualifications, Yearly, 1992). Indeed, referring back to the discussion in chapter 4, it is science that has shown that the environment is not just aesthetic nature but an ecological necessity for human health.

Intangibility creates a rift between experts and laypeople because it means that risks can only be assessed by experts who have the knowledge and the laboratory technology to detect and trace the harms. And while the causal processes may be intangible, the end result certainly is not. People who fall ill due to exposure to harm do feel it, but the explanation for why they suffer remains the territory of scientists.

In *Risk Society* and other works, Ulrich Beck provides an extensive description of the new condition of science. He repeatedly argues that it is science that has made risk knowable, and that when we are faced with risk, more science is routinely called for. But the role of science is also changing. Science, Beck says, is increasingly confronted with its own past, namely the (side effects of) technologies that science itself has fostered. That does not mean that science is discarded, but rather that science is becoming both the cause of and the solution to (and the source of knowledge regarding) risks (Beck, 1992: 155). As we saw in chapter 3, what Beck calls the second modernity is a radicalized modernity, in which the institutions of the first modernity are undermined by their own success. In *Risk Society* Beck argues that science has been successful in that it is heavily used and relied on in many sectors of society. Now, however, science is being called upon to solve problems caused by its own use. Moreover, the public is so exposed to scientific knowledge that it is no longer in awe of science. Science has become entangled with the surrounding society, which means that science also has become politicized and has lost its autonomy. The success of science is that it is being used and understood everywhere today, but this also provokes a crisis for science, namely that it is subject to social and political life in general and has to function within these dimensions. The result is, says Beck, that 'science becomes more and more *necessary*, but at the same time, *less and less sufficient* for the socially binding definition of truth' (Beck, 1992: 156, emphasis in original).

Science (risk assessment), it is often argued, is unable to reflect on the 'unknown unknowns' that might later manifest themselves after a given technology has been put to use. The reason is that short-term scientific tests, focusing on specific causal processes, do not replicate the vast complexity of the ecological system. For example, doing short-term tests for the possible carcinogenicity of a chemical substance by exposing a small sample of laboratory animals to high doses of the substance cannot fully disclose the consequences of large numbers of humans being exposed to small doses over a long time (Tesh, 2000: 27). Furthermore, such tests will not include the possible aggregate effects of a series of chemical substances.

The same complexity creates problems for scientists when they extrapolate from previous results, or laboratory results, in order to predict behaviour in different settings. An example is the nuclear fallout over Wales and Cumbria in the United Kingdom after the Chernobyl accident (Wynne, 1992: 115). Scientists originally predicted that the radioactive radio-caesium rained out on pastures where sheep grazed would be relatively harmless because existing research showed that it would stay in the soil and not be taken up by grass and subsequently eaten by sheep. This unfortunately proved to be spectacularly wrong in the case of the peaty soil of the Cumbrian pastures, and hence the radioactive matter did in fact enter the food chain.

Statistical analysis of human exposure to, say, carcinogens is also fraught with uncertainty. In most cases statistical analysis can only detect the impact of a carcinogen on human health when that impact is substantially higher than the socially and ethically accepted levels of such risk. In others words, there is a considerable gap between those risks that are deemed ethically acceptable and those risks that are scientifically detectable (Hansson, 2002). Lastly, procedure has until recently dictated that regulation or bans could be implemented only when absolute evidence of the danger of a practice, substance or technology was present (Furstenberg, 1990).

Scientific disagreements are frequent, due to the different methodological approaches and designs of experiments. Ottway cites a study in which various scientists were asked to perform risk assessments (Ottway, 1992: 221). Even after they had been given the opportunity to evaluate each other's methodologies and research designs, their findings varied significantly. In other words, differences in framing crop up, both in relation to conflicts between scientific experts and laypeople and to conflicts among scientists themselves (and to conflicts among laypeople themselves, for that matter). A study by Levidow shows that research results on the possible risks of GM crops vary according to how the issues are framed at the outset of the studies (Levidow, 2002). Scientific studies that frame possible cause and effect relations widely (e.g. studies that consider the possibility of insects carrying pollen from GM crops to fields with non-GM crops) tend to generate research results that question the safety of GM crops. These differences have led Webster to argue that differences in framing have much more impact than differences between expert scientists and laypeople (Webster, 2004). Based on these and other arguments, science is often criticized for being too reductionist and too linear, unable to accommodate complexity and uncertainty (Adam, 1998: 35–43, 197). The problem is simply that scientific risks assessments are often framed rather narrowly.

Closely related to this problem is scientists' adherence to the so-called 'null hypothesis'. Take as a hypothetical example scientific assessments of the possible carcinogenicity of substance A. When conducting tests, scientists will normally adhere to the null hypothesis, meaning that from the outset they will assume no causal relation between A and cancer. When conducting tests, scientists can succumb to two types of errors, conveniently called type I and type II errors. They may falsely conclude that A is carcinogenic when in fact it is not (a type I error), or they may falsely conclude that A does not cause cancer when in fact it does (a type II error). Scientists are more focused on avoiding type I errors (falsely abandoning the null hypothesis) than they are on avoiding type II errors (Briggs, 2006). Therefore the null hypothesis is abandoned only when the results are virtually certain, usually meaning results with a probability of truth exceeding 95 per cent. Note that scientific certainty regarding global warming still has not reached that threshold. There are compelling methodological reasons why science needs to progress in this way, but the method obviously carries with it severe disadvantages when it comes to risk assessment. Risks, we have seen, are *possible* dangers. To expect certain knowledge of possibilities is often not realistic. Waiting for scientific certainty in some cases literally means waiting for the risk to materialize into a disaster. Therefore precaution might be beneficial. The costs of banning, say, a possible toxin might be insignificant compared with the costs of having used it, should it later prove to be toxic (Furstenberg, 1990). This way of thinking lies behind the so-called precautionary principle which will be discussed below.

Uncertainty and science

Brian Wynne has outlined a typology of knowns and unknowns comprising four categories: (i) risk, (ii) uncertainty, (iii) ignorance and (iv) indeterminacy. The first, risk, is defined by Wynne in the traditional manner as future dangers which can be statistically calculated. The second, uncertainty, is where there is knowledge about potential dangers but where the probability cannot be established. One might talk of known unknowns. The third, ignorance, applies to cases where the unknowns are unknown. Wynne uses the radioactive fallout over Wales and Cumbria as an example of this. Another, historical, example could be the CFCs mentioned in chapter 1, where for a long time the fact that CFCs destroyed the ozone layer was an unknown unknown (Wehling, 2001). The fourth and last category is where there simply is no knowable or predictable pattern to things – we might call this category unknowable unknowns.

An example such as CFCs shows that there is a time element which is important when it comes to science and risk. Science creates technologies about which the positive effects might be known long before any negative side effect. The process through which unknown unknowns are transformed into known unknowns and from there to known risks is excruciatingly slow. Science takes time – and risk management decisions have to be taken before scientific certainty can be arrived at.

Seeing science as a process also helps to show that while science for all the reasons listed above has severe problems coping with problems of technological side effects, science is no stranger per se to uncertainty. Science is, ideally at least, based on the suspension of commonsensical beliefs. Moreover, science is a process whereby every established certainty itself creates new possibilities and hence uncertainties (Zehr, 1999: 4). Karin Knorr-Cetina, a sociologist of science, talks about scientific activity as the exploration of 'objects of knowledge [which] are processes and projections rather than definite things' (Knorr-Cetina, 2000: 528). Such objects of knowledge are therefore 'unfolding structures of absence', according to Knorr-Cetina – that is, whenever some elements of the object of knowledge are determined, new indeterminate aspects immediately unfold. Engaging with uncertainty, applying wide frames, exploring possibilities are therefore intrinsic to scientific activity, yet it is equally true that the aim of the enterprise is to arrive at viable certainties. Through a painstakingly long (and often recursive) process of theory, empirical testing, debates, peer reviews, publication, paradigm formation and teaching, science is supposed to turn complex uncertainties into scientific facts (at the same time opening up new areas of uncertainty).

This has lead Barry to remark that the problem is not so much scientific determinism but rather the opposite: science is about indeterminist truths while (the risk managing) public authorities want exact information (Barry, 2001: 32). With this we return to the problem of time: concerns about the possible side effects of technology equals concerns about what in the future will be known risks. But the complexity of technology makes science ill-equipped to predict this future.

Another problem is that in spite of science being uncertainty-generating, and even though scientists often arrive at different results, scientists may, when communicating with the outside world, use a wholly different rhetorical style, speaking as if their research results were incontestable (Gilbert and Mulkay, 1984; Zehr, 1999). Wynne gives a vivid example of this when he quotes Grove-White's exchange with a scientist:

G-W: Do you think people are reasonable to have con-
          cerns about possible unknown unknowns where
          GM foods are concerned?

Scientist: Which unknowns?

G-W: That's precisely the point. They aren't possible to
          specify in advance. Possibly they could be surprises
          arising from unforeseen synergistic effects, or from
          unanticipated social interventions. All people have
          to go on is analogous experience with other
          technologies.

Scientist: I'm afraid it's impossible for me to respond unless
          you can give me a clear indication of the unknowns
          you are speaking about.

G-W: In that case, don't you think you should add health
          warnings to the advice you're giving ministers, indi-
          cating that there may be 'unknown unknowns'
          which you can't address.

Scientist: No, as scientists we have to be specific. We can't
          proceed on the basis of imaginings of some fevered
          brow . . . (Grove-White, 2001, quoted in Wynne,
          2002: 469)

Grove-White frames the issue broadly, basing the possibilities of side effects of GM technologies on the fact that other
technologies previously have had such side effects. This is
pushed aside by the scientist as mere speculation. Instead, the
scientist operates with a very narrow frame, focusing on the
actual facts and excluding the future possibilities – that is,
possible unknown unknowns. To the general public such
dismissive statements may seem untrustworthy, given that
scientists evidently often disagree and given that other technologies did prove later to have unknown side effects.

The question is, moreover, whether the public and the
public authorities really do always expect positive scientific
facts. It is at least worth remembering that science produces
a range of (known) unknowns to which most people are
exposed. One example is presomatic genetic screening techniques in medicine, which give people the odds of their suc-
cumbing to diseases in the later stages of life (Novas and
Rose, 2000). Another example would be medical knowledge

of the myriad positive and negative effects of various drugs. This chapter started with an example of this kind, namely hormone replacement therapy. Patients are increasingly exposed to medical practices and expert advice that leave much responsibility with the patients themselves. Leaving such decisions to the individual not only grants freedom but also creates the imperative that one *has* to manage such risks individually. This involves deciding which expert narratives to believe and which risks to take and which to forsake.

Post-normal science and precaution

The dilemma is clear: risk management is reliant on scientific knowledge of *possibilities*. Possibilities are precisely not *certainties*, and there is no time to wait for scientific certainty. Risk management decisions, political or otherwise, therefore have to be made under conditions of uncertainty. The so-called uncertainty principle is a political tool designed for this purpose. In principle, it turns the 'burden of proof' upside down. In the case of our hypothetical substance A, rather than *banning* A only when there is clear evidence that A is harmful, A would be *allowed* only once there is conclusive (or near-conclusive) evidence that A is safe. In practice the precautionary principle is not so strictly enforced, but it is nevertheless a way of reversing usual risk management practice.

Funtowitcz and Ravetz describe these problems by referring to what they call 'post-normal' science (Funtowitcz and Ravetz, 1993). When scientists are faced with risks where there is great uncertainty and where the need for political decisions is urgent, science cannot proceed in the normal fashion, painstakingly gleaning the facts and reporting these to decision makers. In 'post-normal' cases the uncertainties are of such magnitude, and the need for political action so pressing, that it is a better strategy to start not with facts but with values. This does not mean that Funtowitcz and Ravetz believe that science becomes less important in such cases. What does happen, however, is that scientific facts become intertwined with values, and science with politics.

Funtowitcz and Ravetz also point out that over time facts may be established and science may be normalized, but in some cases the experts' risk warnings continue to yo-yo. In such cases effective public policy would be better based on an appreciation of the inherent uncertainties rather than on the illusion that this time science has given us the correct verdict (Funtowitcz and Ravetz, 1993).

Post-normal science is turning things upside down. Political decision-makers and the general public are no longer *given* scientific results (after these have been obtained), they are *demanding* results (which have not been obtained) in order to avoid risks. Moreover, the stakes (political, economic, health) have got higher. With human health and safety in question, science has become subjected to a degree of public scrutiny as never before. Science has been dragged out of its ivory tower and is confronted with questions, demands and criticism from society. And, equally, scientists have themselves left the ivory tower and have engaged in public and political debates, voicing their concerns about possible dangers (Murphy, Levidow and Carr, 2006). Through both these processes, scientific disagreements and scientific uncertainties are becoming more visible. As mentioned before, the scientific disagreements that used to take place in specialist journals have now found their way into the news media.

Nowotny, Scott and Gibbons argue that today's science is both creating more and is more driven by uncertainty compared with past science (Nowotny, Scott and Gibbons, 2001: 34–6). They argue that science has become more intertwined with society, something they call social contextualization of knowledge; but they argue too that as part of social contextualization science has attained a much more entrepreneurial role (in the economic sense) in the knowledge economy. Science has therefore 'gone public' both because it is being held to account politically and because it is used economically more than before. The result is more politicized and commercialized forms of knowledge (Nowotny, Scott and Gibbons, 2001). Nowotny, Scott and Gibbons refer to this new stage of science as mode 2 science. As in Funtowitcz and Ravetz's notion of post-normal science, uncertainty features heavily in the description of mode 2 science. But in the theory of mode 2, 'uncertainty' is understood in a way that is close to the sense in which it is used by governmentality scholars such as O'Malley. Science is becoming, or is involved in, an entrepreneurial enterprise.

The public understanding of science

'Secularization of science' is the term most commonly used to describe how science today is critically questioned rather than blindly believed. Science is undergoing a process similar to that which religion underwent at the dawn of (first) modernity. The result is first of all that the general public regards science with ambivalence. The reason is arguably the inability of science to come up with clear and trustworthy answers in response to public concerns about risk; for instance, during the BSE crisis in Britain, scientists were for a long time unable to provide reassuring answers to the questions of both policymakers and the general public. In a much-quoted government report (*Science and Society*, 2000), the talk is of a public crisis of confidence in science and technology due to the uncertainties and risks that surround new technologies. Rather symptomatically, the problem in the case of BSE was that the UK government based its decisions on early and incomplete scientific results, even though these results proved inconsistent.

The presence of science in the public and political realms means that science is getting tangled up in politics and values. In public debates, conflicting research results and expert opinions are being voiced and used to specific ends, as well as being challenged by laypeople. When it comes to risk, facts are inseparable from values (Schwarz and Thompson, 1990: 23). This is a crucial aspect of post-normal science. Whereas normal science at least could uphold an illusion of political neutrality, as the stakes have got higher science has become more challenged and more 'politically exposed'.

Because science is becoming more politically important and because a lack of information about science can lead to a democratic deficit – and certainly also because distrust of science is a concern – public understanding of science has become a preoccupation of governments around the world, as well as an increasingly important field of study for social scientists. Sociologists and other social scientists have repeatedly pointed out that most political initiatives to improve public understanding of science have been based on what is often called a deficit model. That is, the presumption has been that public distrust of science is merely a question of lack of knowledge and information. The belief is that with more and better information, the public's understanding of risks will fall into line with that of the scientists (for critiques see Felt, 2000; Irwin, 2001). It is worth noting that psychological theories of risk have often been used to support this deficit model; this is because psychological approaches of this kind make it possible to assert that when not given adequate information people are more influenced by (irrational) emotions – that is, that the dread factor attains a higher influence on people's perceptions. One might assume as an alternative, however, that people react strongly to some technologies and practices not because of 'irrational' psychological factors but because these clash with people's values. Wynne has criticized the psychometric approach on these grounds (Wynne, 1989).

The hope that more information would cure the ills of irrationality has been disappointed. Apart from the fact that scientific assessments of given risks both diverge and evolve – something that makes it hard to identify precisely which scientific line the public is supposed to accept – public understanding of science seems to depend also on a range of factors other than strictly cognitive questions of information and knowledge. Psychological mechanisms should not be understood simply as barriers to correct understanding. In spite of attempts to broaden knowledge about science and technology, differences in how much people know seemingly persist (Felt, 2000). As early as 1970 Tichenor et al. argued that increased information flows, most often circulated through the mass media, would benefit those with relatively more education – that is, the more educated would be better able to comprehend information than those with comparatively less education (Tichenor, Donohue and Olien, 1970). Hence the discrepancies in knowledge of scientific matters and risks would increase with increasing publicity. While newer research questions this argument (Bonfadelli, 2005), greater equality does not seem to have been achieved. Another reason why risk communication based on the deficit model has failed to create consensus is, of course, because risks are not objective; they also involve values. So when scientific information about risks is distributed, such information simply triggers, and reinforces, values used to frame the information. Therefore social scientists have challenged the very idea of a *transmission* of objective knowledge to the public, on the grounds that it (falsely) presumes the existence of a pure science that only later becomes entangled with society and the public (Leach, Scoones and Wynne, 2005).

'Luddism' derives from the name of a violent protest movement in early nineteenth-century England, in which textile artisans, known as 'Luddites' (who took their name from the fictive Ned Ludd and were led by 'King Ludd'), revolted against the use of technology in industrial production that took away their livelihood. At times the scepticism among the general public regarding science and technology has been referred to as neo-Luddism. Sociologists and other social scientists studying the public understanding of science can claim as one of their main achievements to have shown how such scepticism is not Luddism, and that it cannot be written off merely as irrational opposition to all things scientific or technological. People tend to frame issues of risk broadly, including questions of values, simply because risks carry a broad range of implications. Laypeople may not be able to evaluate the scientific issues per se, but they both can and do evaluate the degree of transparency and the trustworthiness of the regulatory authorities (Wynne, 1996: 57–8). And doing that is perfectly rational, given the fact that the scientific issues themselves may be incomprehensible. Lastly, most laypeople do not suffer from a misguided perception that the world should be completely risk-free. As Rayner puts it, most members of the public readily accept that all technologies carry risks. What they want is not zero risk but rather trust, liability and consent (Rayner, 1992: 95).

Government attempts to create a better understanding of science have incorporated these insights, seeking forms of communication that build on dialogue. These are clear improvements. Nevertheless, such initiatives in many cases uphold a distinction between values and facts. The democratic aim is for facts and values to come together, but it is still the scientists who are supposed to deliver the facts and the laypeople who are expected to bring the values. Wynne especially has been vocal in criticizing this division of labour. Throughout his work he has sought to show that laypeople's knowledge is also valuable, but is often suppressed by expertise in problematic ways. For example, the experts' advice on how Cumbrian sheep farmers should deal with the radioactive fallout from Chernobyl was largely useless, because it was based on assumptions that simply did not apply to the nature of the soil and the farming methods of those affected (Wynne, 1996). The farmers' own expertise was ignored.

On a different note, and without dismissing the democratic benefits of the initiatives mentioned above, it is clear that such initiatives are part of new technologies of government. As Barry remarks, today each citizen is expected to be knowledgeable about scientific results, so that each individual can take proper and responsible decisions in managing risks (Barry, 2001). In other words, being a scientifically well-informed citizen is one of the ways (quoting O'Malley once again) 'through which we will be expected to govern ourselves; and the ways we will be expected to imagine the world and prepare for the future' (O'Malley, 2004: 7). The example of HRT is of course illustrative in this regard.

'Doing things' with science and risk

Although I have mentioned from the outset that science, in spite the problems just described, has not lost but rather has gained in importance and status, I have been concerned throughout most of this chapter with the problems of science. This does not mean, however, that science is used less today than earlier, or that science and scientific risk assessments are no longer used or are not accepted. In fact they are used more. It is of course beyond the scope of this book to look at the manifold uses of science, but it is relevant to mention briefly how scientific concepts of risk are being used. It is above all governmentality scholars who have studied these usages, and I describe them in more detail in the chapters to come.

Probabilistic calculus of risk (and probability more generally) has been, and continues to be, an incredibly successful technique in relation to a wide range of activities (Short, 1992). Many of these risk assessments are indeed assessments of health and environmental risks, but probabilistic risk technology has also been applied to many other areas.

Insurance as an institution is certainly not buckling under the pressure of the risk society. On the contrary, insurance continues to thrive, although at times the new risks have put insurance companies under severe financial strain (I return to this in chapter 8). Actuarial techniques and knowledge have spread from insurance into fields of government such as criminal justice (see chapter 9). Another example might be road engineering, which involves extensive monitoring of roads and traffic behaviour and where traffic engineers try to minimize the possibility of risky behaviour. I have already touched on medicine. Here, risk as a scientific concept is used not only to assess particular dangers to human health, but also to create a range of preventive and prognostic techniques. People are screened for the likelihood of developing diseases, and huge statistical apparatuses are developed to map causal connections between, say, lifestyle and diseases. Following that come various information campaigns directed at the public. More generally, preventive medicine has become more and more predominant, driven by knowledge of risk. Preventive medicine is today a stellar example of how modern science and medicine govern human minds and bodies, enabled by vast statistical knowledge – what Hacking describes as an 'avalanche of numbers'(Hacking, 1990: 2). Through this, specific 'risk managing subjects' emerge (see chapter 9).

These are brief examples of risk calculations being used. Referring back to the distinction between incalculable uncertainty and calculable risk, we might say that there are more of both in the risk society. As we saw in chapter 3, this question has been the mainstay of the governmentality approach's critique of Beck's notion of the risk society. The argument is that Beck focuses too much on uncertainty (misleadingly calling it risk).

But as the example of insurance shows, scientific notions of risk are used not only in government but also in business. Earlier, when talking about 'science going public' or being 'contextualized', I mentioned that the economic role of science has also increased. This applies also to scientific notions of risk. Drawing on work by scholars such as Stehr (1994) and, above all, Callon (1998), one can talk of the performative power of risk calculations: probabilistic knowledge about risk makes a range of actions, including economic ones, possible. For example, modern finance can be seen as being grounded in the performing of various probability calculations, without which there would be no financial system (MacKenzie and Millo, 2003). By using new probability techniques and computer technology, finance theory has developed a range of highly sophisticated ways of calculating financial risks, which means that such risks can be priced and traded much like insurance policies. Such instruments, known as 'derivatives' or 'structured products', are the biggest part of today's financial systems (Arnoldi, 2004; Lipuma and Lee, 2004). By calculating risks and trading them, risks can become a form of capital, as David Garland states (Garland, 2003: 45, and see p. 151). Finance is also an interesting case because it combines risk and uncertainty. On the one hand, modern finance is built on risk, in the sense of probabilistic calculus, but on the other hand it is all about taking chances, entrepreneurialism and uncertainty. Apparently risk and uncertainty thrive side by side here (and in many other places).

Summary

Many risks, especially environmental and health risks, are surrounded by scientific uncertainty – indeed they are risks precisely because there may be possible, but as yet not fully scientifically established, side effects. Several scientific conventions are ill-equipped for dealing with environmental and health risks. The complexity of the problems, and the time needed for scientific analysis, means that there often are things that science does not know yet. And there are even more things of which the *possibility*, but not the *inevitability*, is known. Scientific results are often inconclusive, contradicted by other scientists and later revised. Science, I have argued, generates uncertainty as well as certainty.

Science has become contextualized; it is part of the economy, of the political and of the everyday as never before. Science generates endless prognoses and probabilities, some of which are mainly applied (e.g. in areas such as finance or medicine), while others are as disputed as they are used (e.g. in areas such as environmental politics). It may seem ironic, but at the same time that science is being confronted with new uncertainties (and hence with its own shortcomings) due to risk, scientific notions of risk, in the sense of calculated probabilities of various harms materializing, have never been more widespread or more in use.

For the average citizen the exposure to science in various contexts has greatly increased in the risk society. In that regard, science has lost it exclusive status. It is often said that the distinct identity of the artist is blurred in the modern affluent society. Artists are no longer members of an elite cultural group, are no longer the only ones who have the time and cultural resources to express themselves aesthetically. Today we all have those means so that we all have become artists. Nowotny, Scott and Gibbons use that as an analogy: today we are all scientists, because we all have the education, the information and the experience to deal with scientific questions (Nowotny, Scott and Gibbons, 2001: 28). While such statements stretch the truth to make a point, science has without doubt been knocked off its pedestal.

Some might bemoan the secularization of science as equalling throwing the baby of modernity – reason – out with the bathwater. But such elitist thinking is probably of limited value, because risks are problems that concern and affect everyone, not just the intellectual elite. A more pertinent worry is that the fusion of facts and values creates a relativism and a disregard for truth that is dangerous in a situation where getting the facts right has never been more important. The contextualization of scientific knowledge means that science is now in the realm of the public, which in practice often means the mass media. The strictly defined procedures and methodological rules that govern science and define scientific truth are often simply drowned out in a medialized public sphere driven by radically different interests. This has serious implications, for instance, for what is seen as valid expertise and what is seen as truth. Different types of expert may operate in this public sphere, no longer reined in by scientific rules. Nowotny speaks of a new type of expert, who is a spokesperson in a hybrid public sphere permeated by both public and economic interests, and whose skills are not only technical but also communicative. Such experts, she writes, have to give accounts that transcend narrow fields of expertise and therefore need collective authority (Nowotny, 2000: 16). The new expert, according to Nowotny, is a mediator (Bauman, 1987; Osborne, 2004), someone who is able to combine technical knowledge with moral and public beliefs. Brown and Michael echo Nowotny when they speak of a transition in expertise from authority to authenticity (Brown and Michael, 2002). With the secularization of science, experts cease to function as authorities with blind followers. Living in the risk society entails the burden of deciding in which expertise to believe (Giddens, 1990; 1991). In taking these decisions, individuals rely on subjective things such as authenticity, which become central valuation criteria. Obviously, this development is closely related to the increased medialization of culture. And as Brown and Michael point out, most powerful positions in society – not only those of experts but also those of politicians, for instance – are increasingly subject to this imperative of authenticity.

Clearly there is a pressing danger of false prophets, and there are clear tensions between the scientific criterion of truth and the mechanism of such a medialized public sphere. Moreover, there seems at times to be a cultural sentiment that amounts to the very idea of truth and scientific proof being viewed with suspicion (Lynch, 1998). No matter what the facts are, someone always seems to be able to claim that they are fabricated or manipulated. The great paradox of the knowledge society is that we have so much information and so little certainty (Lash, 2002; Nowotny, Scott and Gibbons, 2001: 12). However, when it comes to risk, the bottom line is that scientific knowledge alone cannot solve the problems.

I have mainly been concerned in this chapter with the inadequacies of science when it is confronted with highly complex problems that are difficult to model and difficult to predict by extrapolating existing data, and with the uncertainties and scientific conflicts these problems create. I have also touched on the clash between science and the public's argument that when risks are on the political agenda, which they are increasingly often, scientific facts and values fuse. Such an account, however, has a lack: it misleadingly indicates that scientific uncertainty has to do only with the complexity of the subject matter, and that facts and values only fuse when science enters the public domain. This is not completely true. Not only the complexity of the problems but also the different framings of these problems by scientists create conflicting research results and uncertainty. And the only viable explanations for why scientists frame matters differently are that they have diverging professional cultures or that they bring diverging values with them into their field of practice. I shall deal more extensively with both explanations in the next chapter.

6
Risk and culture

The role of culture

In a nutshell, the postulate of cultural theories of risk is that culture, as a set of values and meanings, impacts on how humans perceive risks. This is because these values and meanings (for example, the meaning of 'nature') shape our perceptions of what constitute the biggest potential dangers and form the basis for our reasoning about the solutions. Culture serves as a kind of interpretative 'filter' which influences how humans understand and describe the world. For this reason people have different opinions about what constitutes a risk, just as people have different opinions about many other things in society. Debates about risk are as much about what makes for a good society as about danger in a narrow sense. To try in any way to separate the cultural 'filter' and whatever is being 'filtered' is impossible. The assessments of risk, even scientific assessments, are influenced by these filters from the outset. There is no escape.

The 'filters' are not static givens. They themselves are constantly negotiated through discourse, interaction, political and legal procedures, artistic expression, research and so on, and are affected by economic, technological and political developments. Obviously, different actors struggle over whose interpretations of the world should dominate, and they compete over access to those institutions in society that wield the most influence in these negotiations, such as the mass media or the education system.

Dealing with culture and risk means engaging with a, hopefully not too confusing, mix of difference, sameness and change. People do not necessarily share the same cultural 'filters' and therefore disagreements arise. But neither does each person have a unique filter. Values and ideas are shared – among groups, in institutions and even in societies. For that reason there might be differences among different countries in how risks are handled at the same time that cultural differences exist within each given country. Equally, any given culture may change over time, resulting in changing interpretations of risk.

Risks are socially constructed, yet a great deal of disagreement exists over social constructionism. These disagreements most often turn on how great is the influence of culture and, reciprocally, how big a role 'reality' plays. Some sociologists are rather concerned about statements that all risks are socially constructed, because such statements seem to reduce the real and pressingly problematic nature of problems such as global warming. Such concerns and objections are both understandable and valid. Yet it is perfectly possible to take a moderate stand on social constructionism – simply to say that risks are socially constructed in part. Obviously people do not worry about the same risks. There is thus an element of relativism in play.

Ways of acting, talking and understanding: defining culture

According to the most popular psychological approach, low-probability, high-consequence risks trigger psychological mechanisms that make humans fear these risks more than everyday, statistically more significant risks, such as the risk of a car accident. Other factors, such as risks seeming uncontrollable by the individual, risks being intangible and so on, also might add to what psychologists call the dread factor. BSE and its associated risks must be said to have a high dread factor. Variant Creutzfeldt-Jakob disease certainly invokes fears in most. The threat is invisible yet close by, namely in our food, and therefore seems uncontrollable. No one knows the full extent of the networks for contracting the disease or how long the disease might remain latent in humans. Given these dread factors, it is no wonder that Britain and many other countries experienced much public alarm. But then again, several serious outbreaks of BSE have occurred in Portugal, where, in contrast to Britain and other European countries (including neighbouring Spain), public concern has been relatively minor (Boholm, 2003: 162). The ratio of sick cows to total cattle population in the two countries was about the same, so the risks were comparable in this regard. The psychological triggers apparently 'worked' in some cases, but not others. This indicates that individual psychological mechanisms of risk perception alone cannot explain why some risks become the focal point of relatively great concern and others do not.

What is lacking in the psychometric approach to risk, cultural theories of risk argue, is an account of the cultural fabric that also influences risk perception. Why the Portuguese apparently responded to BSE with much less alarm than, say, the British must be explained by looking at this fabric. Differences in political culture, trust in government, moral values, habits, different media cultures, can greatly influence how much attention a risk receives in public debates and how the public responds.

Explaining differences in risk perception or risk regulation by means of 'culture' might seem like using culture as a 'black box' explanation: if no one knows the reason for something, then it can always be explained by referring to something diffuse, such as 'culture'. Or put differently – how does one describe precisely *how* culture makes a difference, for instance, how culture acts as a perceptual filter? Culture does work in very diffuse and indirect ways, so while one should be wary of black-box explanations, culture must be taken seriously.

Culture affects how humans understand the world because we make sense of the world by cultural means – hence the talk of perceptual filters. Mary Douglas sees culture as values and as systems of symbolic constructs, or, using related terms, *classificatory schemes* (Douglas, 1987: 12) and various *heuristics* (Douglas, 1986: 80), both of which are principles for interpretation and understanding. While most will be able to understand how principles and values affect the perception of risk, terms such as 'classificatory schemes' are harder to intuit. The fact that several other, almost synonymous, terms are used does not make matters easier. Among these are *cognitive schemata* (e.g. Boholm, 2003), *schemata of interpretation* (e.g. Goffman, 1974: 21, 45) or *cultural scripts*, all of which are symbolic constructs that guide and give meaning to actions and rituals (e.g. Alexander and Mast, 2006). Moreover, the notion of *frame*, used extensively in this book, is closely related to schemata (Goffman, 1974). Schemata can be defined as the overall *rules* with which humans make sense of the world. The schema for a circle is hence not a given circle but the rules that determine whether or not a given geometric figure in front of us can be defined as a circle (Luhmann, 2000: 109). More relevant to the case of risk is what I have earlier called frames of expectations: when perceiving risk, we use causal schemata that regulate which possible dangers seem at all possible (see pp. 12–13). Schemata are rules, and hence they include some possibilities and rule out others. Note that schemata are not fixed – they vary and also change. But changes tend to bring crises. Because schemata are rules, they are used to classify things, and they contain expectations and notions about what 'order' is like. One of Douglas's important points is that when the perceived reality forces these classifications and expectations out of kilter, notions of pollution and risk emerge.

It should be clear by now that what unites this plethora of concepts and terms is that they all are used to denote the categories and rules that humans apply to the world in order to make sense of it. That is, the crucial point of convergence of all these rather diffuse terms is that they all refer to *meaning*. How people understand risks – even if risks are understood as such – depends on which meanings are encoded into risks (which meanings are assigned to risks) and, equally crucially, how people interpret risk by using existing meanings (scripts, heuristics, schemata) to decode information about risks. It should also be clear what meaning has to do with culture. As Clifford Geertz writes, culture is a web of signification or meaning which humans have spun themselves (Geertz, 1973: 5). Culture, it follows, influences *how* people make sense of things and *what* makes sense to them. The reason for this plethora of concepts may be in part that various authors use different languages but also that meaning manifests itself in different ways. In this chapter (and in the book in general), I will speak of frames, schemata, values and scripts.

Finally, meaning is ideational, yet it does not exist in the mind of only one person (Geertz, 1973: 10–12). Mary Douglas quotes Durkheim to underscore the point that symbolic categories are social and therefore have more force than if they were merely individual habits:

> The necessity with which the categories are imposed upon us is not the effect of simple habits whose yoke we can easily throw off with a little effort; nor is it a physical or metaphysical necessity, since the categories change in different places and times; it is a special sort of moral necessity which is to the intellectual life what moral obligation is to the will.
> (Durkheim, 1912, quoted in Douglas, 1987: 12)

This also explains to a large extent why culture creates and sustains specific forms of action in society: because of culture, certain ways of acting simply make sense.

The influence of culture, I wrote above, has to do with the meaning with which issues of risk are described (encoded) and understood (decoded). The actors that encode and decode risks bring with them their own particular life experiences and values at the same time that, in their interpretations and actions, they rely on and reproduce both more general cultural scripts and conventions, and scripts and conventions that reflect their social circumstances. For example, research into why people do not always practise safe sex, even though the risk of HIV is well known, points to various cultural factors. In the case of women, for instance, they are pressurized into not protecting themselves by cultural scripts stipulating that they ought to be sexually passive and therefore should not actively plan to have sex and thus should not carry condoms. Another part of this gender script specifies that women should be submissive and trusting of their male partners and hence leave decisions about condoms to them (Parker and Stanworth, 2005). Expert knowledge about the risk of HIV hence contradicts culturally ingrained scripts about femininity.

Individual life experiences, shaped by socio-economic conditions, are also a factor. A study by White of economically disadvantaged African-American women shows how these women exhibit little concern about the risk of HIV and early pregnancies (White, 1999). The reason, White shows, is simply that women from this group see no reason to plan in the long term for a future that holds little promise for them. So instead of protecting themselves they seek immediate pleasure, seeing no reason to avoid early pregnancy, as they have no hope of getting an education or having a career. This once again shows how cultural factors influence, perhaps even override, knowledge about risk. Actions different from what the experts recommend make more sense to the women. Note also that these preferences fit with Douglas's description of the fatalist attitude of the excluded (the upper left-hand corner) in her grid-group model.

Douglas has shown how language as a web of meaning includes the application of binary symbolic categories such as 'pure' versus 'dirty', 'good' versus 'bad', 'natural' versus 'unnatural' and so on. How these signifiers are used might vary between cultures, dependent on tradition. Cheese made from unpasteurized milk might be seen as 'dirty' in the United States but 'natural' in France (Lupton, 2006: 15–16). A very different example concerns the way in which risks have to 'fit into' the web of meaning with which the world is described and understood. Communication about risk does not succeed if the meaning conveyed does not resonate with the symbolic categories and concepts with which humans interpret information. Conversely, some information might be very easily received because it is conveyed in ways that fit very well into the symbolic categories and concepts. One banal example of easily received information might be the possible risks of using mobile phones: scientists have worried about damage to DNA and changes in the blood structure of mobile phone users due to microwave emissions from the phones (Björnstén, 2006). That part of the problem has to do with microwaves has no doubt been a godsend for journalists and others carrying information about this risk into the public realm; they are able to describe the negative effects as mobile phones 'microwaving' the brains of phone users. The meaning of 'microwaving' is immediately recognizable for many people who use microwave ovens, and it conveys a sense of dramatic changes to live tissue. Such news stories resonate with the media audience.

Science and culture

One of the major contributions of Douglas and the colleagues with whom she developed the cultural approach to risk is that of seeing scientific knowledge itself as comprising cultural and political elements. Douglas's collaborators Schwartz and Thompson argue that 'assessments, far from reflecting conflicting evaluations of the facts, involve rival interpretive frames in which facts and values are all bound up together' (Schwarz and Thompson, 1990: 23). This means that scientific disagreements about risks do not simply reflect scientific uncertainty – they also reflect conflicting values. Scientists frame the issues differently and therefore disagree (Levidow, 2002: 846; Schwarz and Thompson, 1990: 56–7). This argument marks a departure from an older school of thought (e.g. Nelkin, 1992), which sees scientific uncertainty as simply a knowledge gap that is subsequently filled by values.

How do scientists frame issues differently? The first of two examples has already been mentioned in passing in chapter 1: in risk assessments of GM agriculture, for instance, a wider framing could include (the possible consequences of) genetically modified pollen being carried long distances by the wind. Including this possibility itself invites new differences in framing, because then it has to be decided the distances such pollen can conceivably travel (Levidow, 2002). As another example, assessments of the possible harmful consequences of Perchlorate contamination in California can only proceed based on estimates of the maximum possible geographical spread of Perchlorate (Briggs, 2006), and on estimates of the greatest possible effect of Perchlorate combined with other chemical substances. These estimates depend on framings.

In discussions of culture and science it is also interesting to note that psychometric research by Slovic and collaborators – although primarily engaged with the differences in risk perception between scientist and laypeople – shows differences in the way in which men and women scientists evaluate the risk of nuclear technologies (Barke, Jenkins-Smith and Slovic, 1997). The female scientists who were surveyed held nuclear technology to be more dangerous than did the male scientists. Gender culture is the only viable explanation.

The arguments about cultural influence on scientific risk assessments represent a rather radical version of social constructionism, which emphasizes culture as a source of scientific conflict and hence uncertainty rather than the complexity of the technology in question. To this one might wish to add a caveat: even though uncertainty is more than a knowledge gap, the complexity involved in assessing the risks of technologies creates a widened array of possible framings. Values and cultural preferences play a big role when scientists engage in such framings, and the existence of a multitude of what Latour and Callon would call associations (technological processes possibly affecting or instigating other processes) makes it possible to frame these issues very differently.

Sheila Jasanoff has repeatedly demonstrated that culture significantly influences the culture of scientific institutions, public understanding of science and the use of scientific expertise to political ends (Jasanoff, 1987; 1997; 2002; 2006). Cross-national differences in expert findings and risk management practices result from this. There are many differences in how risks are conceived of in the United States and Europe. The Americans, for example, view the precautionary principle with distrust. Equally, the use of hormones and GM technology in various agricultural practices is widely accepted in the United States but viewed with suspicion in Europe. The idea that global warming is caused by humans has so far had much less currency in the United States than in Europe, although perceptions are currently changing stateside. One reason for these differences, Jasanoff argues, is different ways of using scientific expertise in government. Even the distinction between what is held to be political and what is scientific is assessed differently in Europe and the United States (Jasanoff, 2002: 373–4). In the United States, Jasanoff argues, a much stricter boundary makes possible the illusion of a disinterested and objective science but also allows for markedly different political conclusions. Modernization, she notes, is not necessarily a homogenizing process – cultural differences still do prevail. In *Risk Society* Beck points out that science itself is far from value-neutral. Rather, science represents a set of values and norms. Moreover, he writes, risks are 'objectified negative images of utopias' (Beck, 1992: 28), and hence the perception of risks is always based on values as much as facts.

The problem with these accounts of how risks and values merge is of course that the precise role and impact of culture remain rather vague. When values intersect with facts, it becomes hard to tell them apart and hence hard to pinpoint the impact of culture. To make matters worse, the impact of culture is rarely direct but rather extremely diffuse. In an older study of how two dioxins were banned as toxic in the United States but not in the United Kingdom, Gillespie et al. state that

> In complex policy issues such as this, where the outcome is determined by the interaction of several causal factors, the roles of cultural and economic factors are diffuse and difficult to evaluate. Their influence is generally mediated through specific institutions and practices, but is, nonetheless, real.
> (Gillespie, Eva and Johnston, 1979: 290)

In other words the influx of culture and values ranges from culturally embedded individual preferences and practices to institutions, conventions and regulated practices such as legal procedures. Such conventions are also reproduced through the mass media, something that I shall discuss later in this book. In their study, Gillespie et al. focus among other things on how different hearings procedures and legal conventions impacted government decisions. I mentioned above that Jasanoff has pointed out similar differences between Europe and the United States (Jasanoff, 1997; 2002). For example, she points out that litigation plays a more important role in the United States than in Europe, that there is a greater emphasis on quantitative risk assessment in the United States and that environmental groups in Europe base their arguments less on science than do their US counterparts (Jasanoff, 1993: 137). These are institutional and legal differences as much as they are cultural, yet they certainly *are* cultural because they are both shaped by and shape general perceptions about what is scientific and what is not, what are collective and political problems and what are not, and what is potentially dangerous and what is not.

Culture, risk and political interest

As we saw in chapter 3, Douglas connects specific understandings of risk with specific forms of organization. A sectarian organization, for instance, will be loosely organized with little structure. In order to maintain group loyalty and a sense of belonging among the members, threats to the sectarian organization have to be created. Here risks are emphasized, and such an organization or group will be both risk-averse and risk-sensitive. An entrepreneurial marketplace, on the other hand, is a loose network of people and does not need an external threat. Hence organizations of this kind might even encourage risk taking. Douglas points out that such differences in the cultural attitude to risk manifest themselves across a variety of risk types. A sectarian community, for instance, shies away from economic risk taking, sees nature as fragile and gambling as immoral. A more entrepreneurial community will, on the other hand, approve economic risk, see nature as robust and also encourage other forms of risk taking, such as gambling (Douglas, 1986: 80).

As described in chapter 3, it is above all the grid-group analysis that makes the relationship between risk perceptions and social organization clear, but Douglas also argues more generally that risks are turned to political account, which often happens by blaming those outside a social group, organization or society. Examples are *ad libitum*. Obviously many so-called NIMBY (not in my back yard) conflicts mobilize communities against a threat from the outside. Those protesting form high group/low grid organizations, for example citizens' groups, with high risk-sensitivity. Equally, the risk of contracting diseases such as HIV might lead to marginalization of certain groups because the central community closes rank. Another example is, of course, the risk of terrorism. Here the risk of terror mobilizes societies by creating a marked distinction between 'us' and 'them'. As Douglas has argued continuously, it is generally the case that risks are attributed to the (deviant) 'other' (see also Lupton, 1999: 123–47).

Examples such as those above make it clear that not only does a central link exist between culture and type of organization, but there is also a link between culture and political interest and power. Indeed, the cultural categories identified through the grid-group model are political cultures (Schwarz and Thompson, 1990: 62). The cultural types represent the four, or rather the three – because the excluded play no role here – main ways of justifying interest and actions. Not only individuals but also political organizations such as interest groups can be categorized according to this model. Seeing the four categories as political cultures makes it clear that disagreements over what constitute the worst dangers are indistinguishable from disagreements over how they should be dealt with. If a given potential danger demands solutions that do not fit a given mode of organization, be it individualist action, hierarchical procedures or sectarian isolationism, the importance of the danger is likely to be played down within the organization and will not resonate much with its members.

Values affect the evaluation of risk. Both people and organizations can change, and people can change their values over time, according to the role and position they occupy in society. Schwartz and Thompson give an example:

> The troublesome critic who finds himself [sic] co-opted by the establishment has travelled in the opposite direction, abandoning the egalitarian and collective fervour of his uncompromisingly activist group for the status and influence of a specially created niche in the administrative or corporate hierarchy. The very success of his organization has enabled him, as its spokesperson or messenger, to argue its case in the august forums that are dominated by those his organization has been criticizing. The more time he spends hobnobbing

with the hierarchs in the corridors of power the less time he has to sit around with those on whose behalf he speaks. It is a difficult balancing act and, somewhere along the way between equality and hierarchy, he finds that he has crossed the hidden line and now has more in common with those who are prepared to make a prestigious place for him than with those who are beginning to ask themselves why they see so little of him these days. (Schwarz and Thompson, 1990: 60)

In *Risk and Culture* Douglas and Wildawsky analyse the way in which the environmental organization Sierra Club became more hierarchical over time, as a result of which the policies of the organization have become more mainstream. This move towards the centre created space for another group, one both more radical and sectarian – Friends of the Earth – which in part spun off from the Sierra Club.

Theoretical arguments such as these do, however, seem to have limits. In the same book Douglas and Wildawsky identify a general cultural change in the United States, which, according to them, means more sectarian values that foster more environmental concerns. Governmentality scholars such as O'Malley have on the other hand identified a general trend towards more individualism and entrepreneurialism (see chapter 3). According to Douglas's grid-group model, more entrepreneurialism would mean looser and less hierarchical social organization with less focus on collective measures against such risks as ecological ones. Maybe it is possible to argue that American society in the 1960s and 1970s became more sectarian, resulting in heightened environmental concern, after which it became more entrepreneurial, which led to decreased environmental concern. But then how does one explain the current heightened concern in the United States over terror, compared with somewhat milder concerns about this particular risk in continental Europe, where environmental concern, especially about global warming, is much more predominant?

One might, to an extent, use the grid-group model to explain these cultural differences and changes (see, e.g., Scott, 1996), but certainly only to an extent. It is clear that different political cultures play an important role in influencing the political decision-making processes and in justifying specific policies – the work by Jasanoff and others mentioned above shows this clearly – but the grid-group model seems too abstract to capture these processes in full. The grid-group gives a good picture of how social context coheres with cultural preferences and how political interests are products of this cohesion. The different and conflicting cultural framings of risks do not simply spring from the four different modes of social organization. Rather, they are moulded through long discursive processes, which the grid-group model is largely unable to describe. The so-called SARF model, on the other hand, seems much better equipped for doing that.

The social amplification of risk

Kasperson and Kasperson developed what they call a social amplification of risk framework (SARF) (Kasperson et al., 2003). The aim is to model the complex processes through which risk is culturally framed in the public domain, leading to some risks being given high importance while others are relatively ignored. Kasperson and Kasperson hold people's perception of risk to be at bottom dependent on heuristics, which are cultural products. They argue that the much broader framing of risks by the public is often valid, but they also maintain that in other cases the end result can be that risks which, seen from the viewpoint of science, are tiny receive unmerited attention while other, better documented risks are ignored. Some risks are amplified; some practices and technologies (nuclear technology, for instance) can indeed be so strongly associated with risk that they are stigmatized (Flynn, Slovic and Kunreuther, 2001).

The notion of social amplification means that information about risk can be 'tweaked' by decreasing or increasing the strength of the 'signal', as well as by filtering the signal, emphasizing certain aspects (i.e. framing it). As a result, information about risk can be either amplified or 'deamplified'.

Kasperson and Kasperson identify various actors or institutions that act as key amplification *stations* and various amplification *steps* (Kasperson and Kasperson, 2005: 105–7).

The stations are:

- scientists;
- risk management institutions;
- news media;
- activists and environmental groups;
- opinion leaders within social groups;
- peer groups; and
- public agencies.

With regard to the amplification steps, Kasperson and Kasperson speak of

- filtering signals (e.g., only a fraction of all incoming information is actually processed);
- decoding the signal;
- processing risk information (e.g., the use of cognitive heuristics for drawing inferences);
- attaching social values to the information in order to draw implications for management and policy;
- interacting with one's cultural and peer groups to interpret and validate signals;
- formulating behavioural intentions to tolerate the risk or to take action against the risk or risk manager; and
- engaging in group or individual actions to accept, ignore, tolerate or change the risk. (Kasperson and Kasperson, 2005: 106)

Kasperson and Kasperson make a schematic representation of this complex process (figure 2). It may be criticized for referring to individual stations, implying that the reception and interpretation of information about risk is cognitive and individual more than it is cultural and social. SARF has in part been developed by scholars from the psychometric tradition, and it is self-evident that psychological factors are important. Fear and dread are in part psychologically grounded. However, one of the arguable strengths of SARF is that it is transdisciplinary, going way beyond psychological

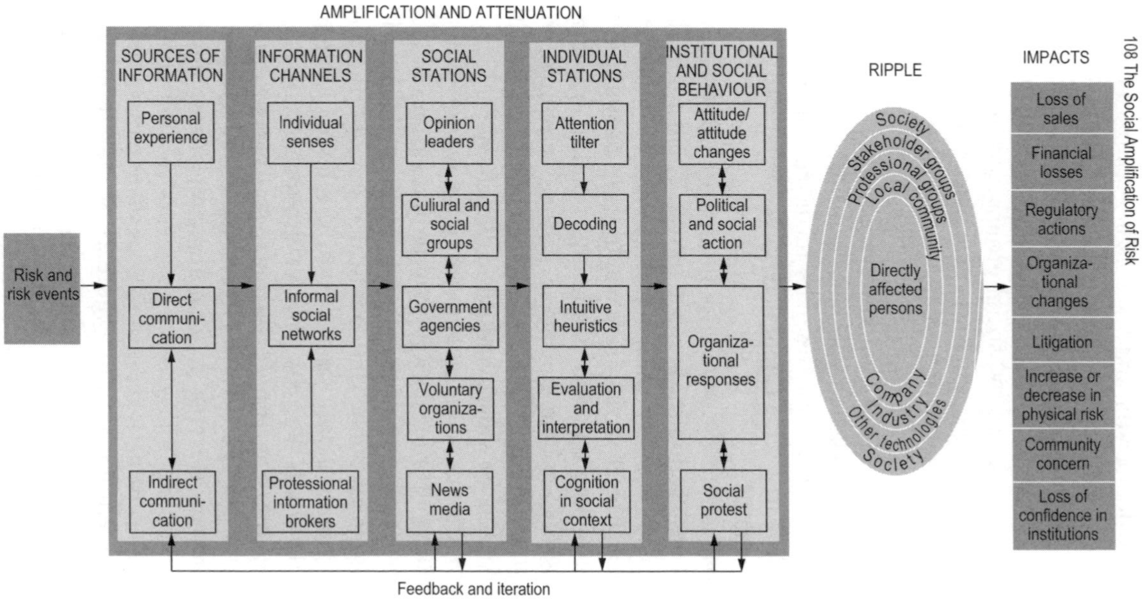

Figure 2. Detailed conceptual framework of social amplification of risk. Kasperson and Kasperson (2005), I, 108, Figure 6.2.

explanations. Kasperson and Kasperson emphasize that the heuristics used to interpret the information are products of culture and therefore social. Furthermore, they maintain that the framing of risk information takes place within, and therefore is also constrained by, social groups and the values of these groups. Kasperson and Kasperson place much emphasis on the symbolic connotations that are created as part of the interpretation of risks. I touched on this above, mentioning how such a metaphor as 'microwaving' might create resonance because it makes the problem somehow recognizable. They also emphasize that the mass media are important in that the media to a wide extent determine the intensity of the information flow.

The social amplification for risk framework takes a moderate social constructionist approach to risk. There are 'real' or objective risks, but through complex circuits of information transmission, objective risks fuse with culture and values. The framework shows that the public and political framing of various risks is a communicative process in which some agents and institutions play a significant role, and in which risks are framed by values and symbolic schemata.

It goes without saying that the framework, with the complex flows of information between the various stations, does not represent in full the process through which various risks attain their public and political status. Furthermore, there is arguably a lack of focus on the discursive power struggles involved. Various interest groups are constantly trying to get their messages and interests through and are struggling for media coverage. Hence one sees advertisements for oil companies trying to brand themselves as environmentally conscious and green movements carefully choreographing their protest actions so that they can secure the most media coverage. Moreover, various political parties and companies try to tap into the 'green' message to increase the popularity of their 'products'. Commercial culture is full of advertising that signifies 'environmentalism' (Linder, 2006) and products that claim to contain 'natural ingredients'. This might be seen as empty rhetoric – indeed, it is – but through such practices the meanings of risk and related things such as 'nature' are also culturally negotiated, and therefore it matters.

Summary

How big the potential dangers are and what should be done about them are two questions that, first, are closely connected and, second, hinge as much on values as they do on facts. What for one person is certain disaster is for another an irrational fear that takes attention way from the – please pardon this deliberately awkward formulation – real potential dangers. The only certainty is that we all worry about some potential dangers. This chapter has investigated some of the ways in which culture influences risk. Central to the chapter are the following: different values and schemata lead to differences in how risks are understood, which risks are seen as especially threatening, and how individuals, communities and organizations manage risks. The cultural negotiation of risk is ongoing; it is a communicative process, a discursive and political struggle over what constitute the biggest risks and what are the best ways of avoiding them. Such negotiations take place under specific social and institutional conditions that influence how risks are framed, and various concepts and meanings are mobilized in order to create resonance. In today's society, these negotiations often take place in the mass media. This raises questions about the inner workings of the media, about who has access to, or can control, the media and about which risks are most easily represented in the media (the subject of chapter 7).

Most of this chapter has addressed cultural and political differences, either between groups in society or between different societies. But culture is not static and the cultural frameworks in which risks are interpreted are not constants – they change with society. This raises the question of whether or not there are cultural traits specific to the risk society, given that 'risk society' refers to changes in, if not new forms of, society. This is discussed in chapter 8.

7
Risk and the mass media

The media and perceptions of risk

We are all familiar with so-called 'media scares' – stories about risks that erupt in the mass media. The fact that media scares are so familiar is probably the best indicator of how great an impact the mass media have on the public perception of risk (Barry, 2001; Koné and Mullet, 1994; Tulloch and Lupton, 2001: 48). The media not only have a significant influence on risk perception (see, e.g., Slater and Rasinski, 2005), but also have a huge impact on contemporary culture more generally (Thompson, 1995). The impact of the media on culture must always be understood, however, as part of a complex and recursive relationship. It is difficult to ascertain whether media discourse mirrors cultural trends or whether the media to a significant degree have produced such cultural trends.

In the social amplification of risk framework (SARF), discussed in the previous chapter, mass media were one of the key stations in the transmission of information. The SARF has, however, been criticized by media scholars (e.g. Hughes, Kitzinger and Murdock, 2004) for offering too simplistic a view of the mass media, as simply a societal institution that transmits information. The SARF, it is argued, ignores the diversity of media and the unpredictability of media perception. It is true that the mass media in the SARF are reduced to one element in a schematically represented communication process which in reality is highly complex. It is therefore worthwhile to look in more detail at the mass media, but this does not mean, I argue, that the SARF ought to be dismissed altogether. The idea of amplification and de-amplification will therefore be maintained in what follows, but the hope is to give a much more nuanced account of the role which the media play in amplification processes.

A good way to start is by discussing why and how the mass media are important SARF stations. When it comes to both the influence on culture generally and the influence on risk perception specifically, the exact dynamics of media power are difficult to pinpoint. There are many reasons why that is, but two arguably stand out. First, we are all exposed to vast amounts of media information, and this information becomes part of our knowledge about the world. But media information not only becomes part of our knowledge, it also influences how we subsequently understand – I have discussed this earlier, using the concept of framing – information we later receive and how we reappraise things we know already (see Eldridge, Kitzinger and William, 1997). The mass media, in other words, not only provide information, they also, simultaneously, frame issues which influence how other information is being interpreted (Kitzinger, 2004: 15–16). The media hence have both a direct and an indirect influence on risk perception, which cannot be easily separated. For example, media coverage of the risk of smoking may influence how actors interpret other information about the same risk just as much as it may provide new factual knowledge about these risks.

The second dominant reason why media power is a diffuse subject is that not only are the media diverse, but people's perceptions of media information also differ widely (Anderson, 2006). At first glance, the finding that media reception is heterogeneous is inconsistent with the proposition that the mass media exert great influence over people. For the media to have impact they ought to affect people in at least relatively uniform ways. This seeming contradiction may, however, be explained. The media audiences use their already ingrained values and cognitive frames when making sense of the imparted information, and they of course view the information on the basis of the context in which they find themselves (Sturgis and Allum, 2004). A good deal of the power of mass media lies in the fact that that they trigger already ingrained beliefs. The mass media in other words do have a strong impact, but that impact may often mean that cultural differences are accentuated. Communication, media studies teach us, is not a linear transfer of information from a transmitter to a receiver. In chapter 5 I also mentioned that differences in the level of education in the media audience may lead to even bigger differences in how information is perceived. Tichenor et al. (1970) have, for example, argued that more media coverage of complex health risks could increase the knowledge gap between well- and poorly educated people because the former had the cultural and educational resources necessary to comprehend the information while the latter did not. Newer research questions the simplicity of this proposition but nevertheless finds empirical evidence that there are significant social and cultural differences in how mediated information is interpreted (Bonfadelli, 2005) – differences which can create knowledge gaps.

Analysis of the public understanding of science has to involve the mass media, not only because the media convey information about science to the public but also because the media constitute the forum in which such information is discussed and debated. In other words, the contemporary public sphere is predominantly a medialized public sphere (Schulz, 1997; Thompson, 1995: 131–2). For that reason environmental groups and community leaders, along with several other of the key actors listed by Kasperson and Kasperson as 'stations' in the SARF framework, seek access to, and influence on, the mass media. The mass media are increasingly becoming a 'meta-station', one could say – a station to which it is vital that actors from the other stations have access (Arnoldi, 2007; Couldry, 2003). Correspondingly, many of the amplification steps ultimately happen in the media. Actors with a political stake in the public discussion of risks will seek to influence the perception of risk by promoting their own frames and encoding risk issues (Stallings, 1990).

Based on this, one may roughly distinguish between two forms of media power. The first type has to do with the media being central stations or 'valves' in the information stream, letting some information flow while simultaneously cutting off other information. The world is made available to us through the media and the media set the agenda. As a consequence, there is great power in being among those who control these 'valves'. The second form of media power is due not to the quantitative flow of information but rather to the encoding or framing of information. Meaning encoded by the mass media has a far-reaching impact on the surrounding culture. The frames, styles, aesthetics, values and narratives (in short, media discourse) of the media rub off on all of us (Schudson, 2003: 27), albeit in different ways. To speak in grand terms, the media are powerful cultural machines.

It is important to remember that, in the amplification processes in the media, moral values and political interests fuse with fears of risks. For example, using the language of Mary Douglas, various practices which are peripheral to, or threaten, the centre's values may be described in the media as risky rather than simply deviant or morally corrupt. The phenomena which are perceived as risks, Douglas reminds us, tend to come from the edges of or outside culture. An example might be the media coverage of techno raves, where the risk of drug taking, which often follows, is highlighted (Hier, 2002). Such coverage oscillates between moral condemnation of the excesses of the young and setting out the risks of such excesses. Another example could be obesity, wherein accounts of the health risks related to obesity are given moral undertones suggesting a lack of self-control and so on (Lupton, 2004). Obviously, the power of the media also makes them important technologies of government. Mass-mediated discourse is central to creating specific subjectivities. An example might be the many pages of health coverage in newspapers and magazines, where subjects learn to manage their lives healthily by becoming aware of, among other things, the risks of lack of exercise, drinking alcohol, eating fatty foods. I return to this later.

Perhaps inevitably, there is a strong tendency to focus on the mass media's tendency to amplify the scale of risks rather than focusing on those instances where the mass media de-amplify (or simply ignore) risks. Several media scholars are highly critical of the mass media for promoting a culture of fear (Altheide, 2002; 2006) for reasons of sensationalism and commercial interests, and as a result creating media scares about the risks of technologies such as mobile phones, but also other risks such as that of crime. This criticism is primarily directed at news media, the inner logic of which is worth investigating for that and several other reasons.

Bad news is good news

Giving a precise definition of news media has never been easy, but the Internet has made it even harder. Much information, including information about risks of different kinds, is circulated on the Internet, often as peer-to-peer communication. This means that on the Net there often are no 'information gatekeepers'. This is a marked contrast to the traditional news media, where editors decide what is newsworthy, and where professionally trained journalists cover the selected news stories according to professional conventions. As a medium, the Internet has enhanced the possibility of communication between laypeople and in this sense is arguably the first true mass medium. This is on the one hand the great promise offered by the Internet, that no one can control the information and it has been freed from the interests and influence of a select elite; this promise is on the other hand also its greatest weakness. The Internet contains an excess of information, the validity of which is hard to assess because it is hard to determine who the senders are and if these senders are biased or themselves have been manipulated, or simply are not trained to assess and impart information. Perhaps because of these weaknesses much news on the Internet is today conveyed by 'traditional' news organizations such as newspapers or television stations that now also have outlets on the World Wide Web. This indicates what type of media this section will be dealing with, namely media outlets that produce 'news', a specific category of information that has a specific form (or at least a specific range of such forms), is being 'produced' by a specific profession and as such has a specific validity.

For stories about risk to be covered in the news media they must first of all be newsworthy. Journalists and editors both consciously and unconsciously in deciding what constitutes news act according to professional criteria; among these are magnitude, surprise, proximity and impact. Magnitude means that, say, big disasters are more newsworthy than small accidents. Unexpected events, happening for the first time, are also newsworthy. And events happening nearby, and/or those that directly affect many of the news recipients, are more newsworthy than those happening further away. These news criteria themselves amplify or de-amplify risk. The risk of car accidents is less newsworthy than the risk of, say, nuclear accidents. The potential magnitude of the latter, and the simple fact that there are fewer of them, means that their news value is higher, and this even though many more people die in car accidents each year, meaning that the objective risk of the latter is much greater.

The example is simple and might seem unnecessarily grim, but another fact about news value is that stories about bad things happening generally have high news value. There are of course obvious exceptions – a story about, say, a baby being saved thanks to the heroic efforts of a stranger is undoubtedly a good news story – but generally the rule is that seen from the point of view of editors, bad news is good news (Schudson, 2003: 49). Risks as they have been described in this book, namely as potential high-impact dangers, often receive great media attention because they satisfy many of the news criteria.

An alternative way of thinking about how the news media select and produce news bears heavily on Mary Douglas. Culture for Douglas is a set of expectations and norms that define what is normal, expected and acceptable. Risk, on the other hand, is for Douglas that which throws our understanding of the normal and the expected out of kilter. In today's societies it is to a large extent through the media that expectations and norms are maintained and produced. The news media therefore react when expectations about normality – be it moral expectations about the behaviour of humans or scientific expectations about technology – are breached (Luhmann, 2000). They do so in order to create new expectations and hence re-establish a sense of what is normal, or to reinforce the existing cultural order by identifying the causes of and blaming those responsible for the breaching. This leads to a slightly alternative theoretical explanation for why stories about risks often hold great news value: risks are events which break with collective cultural conventions about normality, and news media coverage serves either to reshape or to uphold (through moral condemnation) existing conceptions of the normal in the face of such events. By the same token, risks which are insoluble and permanent tend to become viewed as normal and lose news value.

News stories about risks will often try to identify a guilty or responsible party. A key element in the professional self-identity of journalists is the idea of the journalistic profession being the fourth estate. Journalists traditionally see themselves as public watchdogs and believe that they have a democratic function as such. One of their roles as watchdogs, at least in theory, is to expose those who put the general public at risk or in other ways violate or disrupt the legal or normative order. For that reason stories of risk will often focus on who is to blame. Have greedy executives withheld information or knowingly exposed the public to risk? Did incompetent regulators or politicians fail to protect the public? Such questions are often posed in news stories. Again this relates strongly to Douglas's work on risks and blame, and underscores how the mass media in today's society have a key role in creating the cultural cosmology which holds society together.

An example which sheds some light on several of the dynamics just discussed could be the coverage by British news media of the risk of salmonella infection caused by the undercooking of poultry. Initial coverage of this risk focused heavily on the responsibility of the producers who had failed to provide consumers with germ-free poultry. But gradually experts came to focus more on the responsibility of consumers, who, it was argued, were expected to maintain a necessary level of kitchen hygiene and cook the poultry to a temperature which would kill the bacteria. Once that expert discourse became dominant, the news media lost interest in the issue (Hughes, Kitzinger and Murdock, 2004: 257–8). This example illustrates, first, how news media find it difficult to cover risk stories where blame cannot be attributed to a specific person or group. Once the culprit became the general public the media could no longer use a specific form of news discourse which would identify and condemn the outside creator of a potential danger. Second, the example shows what happens when a danger becomes permanent and the finger of blame is no longer pointed; then danger becomes normal and ceases to be news.

The propensity to attribute blame to an outside cause manifests itself in various ways. Media coverage of the risk of smoking might, for example, focus excessively on whether or not cigarettes contain additives that enhance addiction rather than on the simple danger of smoking. This enables the media to attribute blame to a few tobacco producers rather than to smokers more broadly. Yet there are of course issues with regard to which it is virtually impossible to attribute blame. Global warming, which in many ways can be said to everyone's fault, does not fit easily into this narrative structure. This does not, of course, mean that problems such as global warming do not feature in news stories but it is no doubt an obstacle to the coverage of that particular risk. News stories are narratives with specific discursive structures (Dijk, 1985; 1988a; 1988b), and some news items fit these structures better than others.

The media have several other traits which affect the coverage of risk. Staying with global warming, we observe that the modern media have created a visual culture with its own possibilities and constraints. Dunlap notes that global warming suffers from the fact that it is difficult to represent visually, a problem in a culture that in particular is becoming more and more visually medialized (Dunlap, 1998). The news media also tend to focus on single events rather than on a series of (repeat) events (Schudson, 1995: 55). No news stays new. Because of that, media interest tends to wane unless new things happen. Perhaps for that reason, media attention to environmental issues such as global warming tends to be cyclical, repeatedly increasing, stagnating and decreasing (Hansen, 1993; McComas and Shanahan, 1999). McComas and Shanahan show how, in those stages of the cycle where attention to global warming is growing, news stories focus on the negative consequences of the given risk (McComas and Shanahan, 1999). In periods of stagnation or decreased media attention, the focus is instead on scientific disagreement. This reflects the media's news criteria. While the initial consequences of a possible risk are news (magnitude, effect on people), these possible consequences cannot stay news for ever, and instead conflicting expert opinions become news, albeit to a lesser extent, which means that interest stagnates and finally wanes. The process might then repeat itself if and when the potential danger becomes more manifest and/or the results of new research shed new light on the issue.

However, the media's search for fresh news might not alone explain the cyclical variations in media attention. Mazur argues that differences in media attention also vary according to the extent of social connections between journalists and sources – changes might occur when politicians who are able to put the environment on the agenda are elected, or when scientists with good connections to journalists publish new research results or are promoted (Mazur, 1998). Moreover, centrally placed science journalists – that is, science journalists working for the central news agencies or for leading news outlets – exert great influence over the media coverage of risk (Meek, 2002). Their retirement or career changes might also account for some of the variations in the media's risk coverage over the years (Mazur, 1998).

News is in other words the product of long chains of inter-action and communication between sources and journalists rather than simply events that take place in the world. Many actors influence, or seek to influence, what features in the news and what does not and how the selected news items are covered. Many of the technological risks are highly complex, and it can be difficult for journalists to get to grips with them. For the same reason, much of the media coverage of such stories depends on a few science journalists who have consid-erable influence on news coverage. Coverage of complex risk issues stemming from technology often mean that journalists will have to base their stories on expert sources, something which poses a range of difficulties for journalists. Even science journalists often have difficulty in evaluating the scientific merits of the experts and their statements. The relationship between journalists and experts is in many cases lukewarm at best, as journalists find scientists inaccessible while scientists in turn find journalists superficial and sensationalist (Peters, 1995). One major reason for this is that scientific knowledge – not least when it comes to risk issues – is often fraught with uncertainties. As a result, scientists present research findings with caveats. Journalists, on the other hand, have no use for caveats; they want clear-cut information (Stocking, 1999). Another area of dissonance between the two professional cultures is that journalists often frame issues much more broadly than scientists; for instance, journalists are apt to raise moral concerns (Malone, Boyd and Bero, 2000), while scientists focus on the scientific aspects only.

Competition and commercialization

The sum of all this is that journalistic coverage of risks is influenced, often even partly hindered, by a series of factors. The risk issue in question often has to be relatively new and hitherto uncovered and it must have magnitude and pose danger to a broad section of society. And, whenever possible, the people responsible for creating the risk or not curbing it should be identified and criticized. But if the risk is relatively new it will almost invariably be clouded by uncertainty. Journalists are then faced with the difficulty of covering the issue in such a way that the relevance of the issue remains clear while still giving a balanced account – and this based on sources which are sceptical of all attempts to reduce the complexity of the issue and unwilling to engage in the often political discussion about who is to be blamed and whether actions to reduce the risk are justified.

These are not easy working conditions and, to complicate matters further, journalists face competition both internally and externally. Their story competes with many other stories for the attention of the editors and prominent placement in the newspaper or broadcast (or placement at all). And externally the specific news outlet competes with other news outlets in producing the most sought after and agenda-setting news. On both fronts, certainty, relevance, magnitude, proximity, responsibility and other news criteria are crucially important. The problem in many cases is that when it comes to news coverage the potentiality, uncertainty and ambiguity of risk have to be toned down. Either a risk is truly and surely dangerous or it is not news at all.

Increased competition in the news media industry has only accentuated this. The mass media and the news media – which continue to be the focus here – have indeed changed tremendously. Not only have new media such as the Internet and digital television and radio emerged, the news media have also changed radically in terms of market structures, ownership, audience and distribution. The media landscape of most west European countries of the 1950s and 1960s was dominated by national public-service news stations – epitomized by the BBC in Britain – and by national broadsheets. In the United States things were slightly different (see Nerone and Barnhurst, 2003), among other things because there were few broadsheets with a truly national distribution and no national public-service institutions in the European mould. But nevertheless broadsheets such as the *New York Times* and television networks such as CBS were dominating the media market, hence playing roles comparable to those of the European public-service stations and national broadsheets, at least in terms of journalistic style and influence.

Since the 1970s this media landscape has been dramatically altered. Media markets have been deregulated, creating not only many new outlets but also multinational media conglomerates. As a result the public-service stations find themselves in competition, as do the traditional broadsheets. There is an ever increasing number of commercial television and radio stations and the market for printed news is also being transformed, the newest addition in Europe being free newspapers such as *Metro* that are financed by advertisements.

These changes go way beyond ownership, since they also affect the content and format of news. Broadly speaking, both electronic and printed news have become more commercial, and as a result also more sensationalist, but such claims always need to be followed by the important caveat that while the tabloid news format to some extent has prevailed, so has diversity. News today comes in a range of genres and formats hitherto not seen, ranging from small niche outlets catering for select audiences to broad commercial news productions. These can increasingly be accessed across national boundaries, thanks to satellite transmission and computer networks, the same technology which makes it possible to produce news in a variety of formats.

However, returning to the question of sensationalism, it is arguable that while news comes in a variety of formats and a multiplicity of outlets, it is often the same news. Commercial news outlets employ relatively few journalists and instead rely heavily on news agencies to provide news stories. As a result, news outlets tend increasingly to disseminate the products of a few news agencies that deliver to many such outlets. This centralization of news production is indeed often accentuated when it comes to stories about risk which involve technology and science. When dealing with such stories with a complex subject matter, editors of newspapers with a small staff are often forced to rely on the news agencies which employ specialized science journalists. As a result, these science journalists can effectively dominate the coverage of these topics (Meek, 2002). The competition among the many different news outlets in the market also creates a tendency to imitate. Editors often find it impossible to ignore the lead of the day from the news agencies, fearing that if they were to do so they would lose out to their competitors. The competitors in turn think the same, and hence all cover the same story. As a result, particular stories, for example about risk, get a lot of sudden attention while other stories are ignored. Increased media competition and diversity, in other words, do not reduce the media's propensity to amplify some risks and de-amplify others. The competition to create attention-generating headlines may of course also cause some form of sensationalism. Sensationalism remains, however, a dubious term, I argue, if only because it smacks of elitism. But it seems obvious that news outlets facing stiff competition seek to promote their news by creating attention-generating headlines and describing events that stir emotions such as fear. Hence some risks, for example the risk of crime, may receive much media attention and be covered in ways which accentuate the risk (Altheide, 2002).

The media, health and lifestyle

Content analysis of the *Washington Post* which I carried out some years ago showed that the word 'risk' (including its plural form) appeared in 1,327 articles in 1977 and 4,784 articles in 2000 (Arnoldi, 2003). To a wide degree, though not exclusively so, this significant difference was due to an explosion of the usage of the term 'risk' in the health section of the paper (it should be mentioned that the difference in the overall output of articles and their length between the two years was marginal). This difference between two selected years might be coincidental, but very likely it is an indication that a gradual preoccupation with personal health which included a strong preoccupation with risk had occurred between those two years. The mass media both influence and mirror contemporary culture. Looking at changes in news media (and hence by extension at culture), one of the most profound changes when it comes to risk is indeed the amount of news about how one as an individual can stay healthy. Many newspapers today, for example, have a weekly 'lifestyle' and/or 'health' section with a heavy focus on health and healthy living and in such sections there is much emphasis on risk.

This type of coverage deals with nutrition, sports, lifestyle, pharmaceutical drugs and their benefits and side effects, alternative medicine and much more. And risks are discussed almost everywhere, for example with regard to smoking, not exercising or eating saturated fats, or, to the contrary, the risk-reducing properties of, say, 'superfoods' or exercise are featured. On television there is a variety of programmes that deal with nutrition, obesity or diet – often chronicling specific attempts by individuals, aided by various experts, to lead a better and more healthy life. The mass media hence offer the clearest reflection of a remarkable change which has happened in recent decades and which has made the individual conduct of one's own health a pressing concern. This particular type of media coverage differs from the risks stories which I have described so far. Here, the issue is not potential dangers of great magnitude but instead the 'best practices' by which the unavoidable dangers of living can be reduced as far as possible. Here risk is not the primary issue but rather a concept by means of which strategies for managing one's body and future (or rather the future of one's body) can be discussed.

Expert sources also feature heavily in this sort of media coverage, but uncertainty is less of a problem here compared with the risk stories discussed previously. And when uncertainty is an issue, for example in regard to the possible side effects of a pharmaceutical drug, the point of the news item is clearly to provide as much knowledge about the pros and cons as possible, so that each individual can make the best possible decision.

This type of media discourse no doubt contains many and diverse aspects, of which several have little connection to risk. We may for instance say that television documentaries about, say, obese people struggling to lose weight (or struggling with any other problem they might have) provide people with a chance to identify with others and their struggles and gain a sense of belonging. But a significant part of what is at hand is a media discourse which, often focusing heavily on risk, creates an emphasis on individual responsibility (Rose, 2000: 327). What is at hand here is a cultural and moral narrative according to which we all can, and should, control ourselves in order to be, in this case, healthy and active people. We are observing media discourses here which aim to conduct the conduct of others, that is, in Foucaultian terms, an 'ethical' form of governance which seeks to make subjects conduct themselves in certain ways. In this case the responsibility is in regard to health and healthy behaviour, but, as we shall see in coming chapters, the ethical governance centres not only on health but also on 'financial' prudence, sexual behaviour and many other things. And all of these with strong moral overtones.

The governmentality tradition mostly focuses on the actions and governing techniques of state institutions such as schools, hospitals or prison facilities. But there is no reason why the mass media should not also be included. After all, political theorists have increasingly come to see the mass media – although they in many cases have been privatized – as political institutions (Cook, 1998). Foucault's work on governmentality also stresses that power resides not at one place but at many. In this sense it is entirely reasonably to include the news media as one of the power-yielding institutions of modern society. However, the governmentality tradition does not really lend itself to the idea that there is a direct confluence of interest between state and private enterprises. Power, seen from the point of view of the governmental tradition, is much more non-linear and heterogeneous than, for example, Marxist thought about ideological hegemony would hold.

Conclusion

I began this chapter by arguing that the mass media constitute an especially important station in the social communication processes which Kasperson and Kasperson describe using the notion of the SARF. The reason is that much information and many of the frames with which we perceive information and form expectations are imparted to us by the media. I subsequently attempted to describe in more detail the diversity and the complexity of the mass media with a strong focus on the news media and their coverage of risk issues. I showed the various difficulties experienced by the mass media when faced with risk issues, difficulties with representing the complexity of the issues. Such an analysis might be taken to mean that the mass media are wholly inept at representing and imparting information about risks – something which obviously would be a serious problem – but this is not really the point. The point is rather that the media are struggling with the complexity and uncertainty of risks issues just as much as are other institutions in society (science being no exception), not to mention individual human beings. Risks are often uncertain because they elude both lay and scientific frames of expectation and because their interpretation hinges on values. Hence different media outlets will often interpret risks differently according to their political leanings. We are in many ways dealing with issues here which are similar to what was discussed in chapter 5 regarding science: just as is the case with science, there are professional norms and frames institutionalized in the media which create specific difficulties regarding risk coverage.

Having perhaps focused unduly on how the media might distort – that is, either de-amplify or amplify – risks, it must also be stated that the mass media are important because they are the means for creating political and cultural change, including new awareness of risks and ecological problems. The mass media can create, and have created, new awareness and new political movements in relation to risk issues. This important aspect – indeed, the great political potential of the media – is not adequately grasped if the discussion centres on social amplification (or de-amplification) of risk. Faulty, distorting, commercialized the mass media may be, but they nevertheless create public spheres and movements within and across national borders (Silverstone, 2007).

The mass media are also, I argued above, 'cultural machines', conveying new cultural narratives or reinforcing existing ones. In terms of the current focus on health and risk, it seems evident that we are witnessing the emergence of a cultural narrative which implicitly stipulates that humans are expected to take responsibility for their own health and well-being. As I have already written, this extends way beyond health and health risks. It is connected, I shall argue in the coming chapters, with a general cultural narrative that celebrates individual control. What is valorized is the notion that human individuals are capable of steering themselves through uncertainties and dangers. This cultural narrative – something which I also referred to at the end of chapter 6 – is manifest in several ways, one of which is the obsession with health (and individual control thereof). Other examples are celebrations of the entrepreneur and the successful financial speculator, the person taking calculated risks in extreme sports, the successful high-stakes gambler and so on. The next chapter will further analyse this new cultural narrative, which celebrates controlled, prudent and above all successful risk management and even risk taking.

8

Risky futures: pleasure and capitalism

Climbing mountains

'Green Boots' is a macabre landmark. It is the name given to the frozen body of a climber who died on Mount Everest on 10 May 1996, close to the summit. The dead man's real name is unknown, but he is believed to be Tsewang Paljor, one of three Indian climbers who all vanished on the mountain that day. Ever since, his frozen body has lain curled up under an overhang by the side of the trail leading up to the mountain's peak. It is far from the only body on Everest. Climbing Everest has developed from an undertaking for only a few highly trained mountaineers to an industry proper, with many companies offering tours. More than 1,500 people have now reached the summit of Everest, including a person aged 70, a blind person and one person who had both legs amputated after suffering severe frostbite on an earlier attempt. A couple has been married on Everest. With Everest becoming ever more popular, both the physical capabilities and skills of the climbers have come to vary more and more. As a result – and because China's liberalization has meant that the northern, more dangerous slope of Everest has become accessible, and at much lower prices than the southern slope controlled by Nepal – the death toll is rising steadily. To this day more than two hundred people have died trying to reach the summit of Everest. On 10 May 1996 alone, ten people vanished in a severe storm. As if that were not enough, the story of Green Boots has since taken an even more shocking turn. On 15 May 2006 a British climber, curled up against Green Boots, died from hypothermia while at least forty other climbers passed by him. He did receive some help from some of the climbers, but apparently most of them simply passed by. Several of the latter defended themselves by saying that they had mistaken the dying Briton for Green Boots. These events sparked worldwide outrage, with much finger-pointing in various directions. One person blamed was the legless man mentioned above – he was one of the climbers who saw the dying Briton during his own successful climb, accomplished on prostheses. But in spite of this outrage, 'the circus', as Sir Edmund Hillary has described the contemporary Everest climbing industry, will continue, and more will die trying to reach the summit.

Obviously climbing Everest is risky. It is an example of what Stephen Lyng has called edgework (Lyng, 1990). The notion of edgework is the most established theoretical conception of voluntary risk taking. Lyng has taken the term from gonzo journalist Hunter S. Thompson to describe activities that put at risk 'one's physical or mental well being or one's sense of an ordered experience' (Lyng, 1990: 857). Like other forms of edgework, mountain climbing is surrounded by a particular narrative, what Lyng calls *vocabulary of motive*, of personal development by overcoming extreme physical challenges and risks (Ortner, 1997: 139–40). Equally there is a strong narrative of skill. Self-descriptions of such activities always emphasize the importance of personal skills, Lyng argues – for instance, the physical skills of a rock climber or the ability to keep a cool head when skydiving. In this narrative, surviving (in this case, Everest) is not about having luck with the weather and equipment or being able to pay for guides and Sherpas. The emphasis is instead on physical skills, the mental toughness to endure and the ability to make the right decisions under severe pressure.

This chapter will deal, among other things, with voluntary risk taking. Most of what has been discussed so far in this book has to do with avoiding risk. Yet here the topic is the increase in activities organized around the taking of risks and a correlating cultural narrative in which risk taking – be it skydiving, poker playing or business entrepreneurship – is glorified.

Even though we are dealing here with voluntary risk taking, this does not prevent blame from being attributed when things go wrong. Relatives of people lost on Everest have, for instance, sued guiding companies for putting their relatives at risk. It has also been argued that people have died from using recycled, and therefore malfunctioning, oxygen tanks rather than simply from exposing themselves to danger. Attribution of blame is thus one trait of risk discussed so far, which applies also to edgework and voluntary risk taking. But the question is, of course, how the idea of edgework and other notions of voluntary risk taking relate to the idea of the risk society discussed up to this point. The answer is that, above all, voluntary risk taking, according to Lyng and others (Baker and Simon, 2002; Reith, 1999; 2005), is a practice that has become much more prominent since the late 1960s. In other words, the rise of edgework coincides with the emergence of the risk society. This more than anything else indicates that voluntary risk taking is not separate from, but rather is complementary to, the risk society as it has been discussed so far.

Edgework, individualization and entrepreneurialism

Voluntary risk taking is an important field of study, and with the notion of edgework a theoretical framework has developed that is important in its own right. Yet there are also obvious links between voluntary risk taking and other aspects of risk, which can be theoretically explored. Drawing on Marx and Mead, Lyng argues that edgework is becoming popular because it allows the actors to seek refuge from the alienating structures of modern society. Lyng sees edgework as a set of practices and a narrative that allow the individual self to take control and to feel that individual skills and individual action matter more than random or distant forces. Outside edgework, there is often no place in modern society for this construction of the self as being able to control and influence events. Not surprisingly, edgework is often described in terms of personal development. Edgework means overcoming the group and the routines of social life, overcoming fear and other weaknesses and evolving as a person.

Part of the edgework narrative is the idea of personal fulfilment – that exposing oneself to danger creates self-confidence and personal growth. Herein lies a link to ideas about the construction of the reflexive self (Giddens, 1991: 5). There, the focus would be on the narrative of personal development through edgework. This allows for the construction of self-identity, which increasingly is something one must piece together and plan for, as tradition and community no longer automatically confer it.

McGuigan has used Beck's notion of individualization to argue that contemporary culture is a risk culture, not, or at least not only, in the sense that it is a culture influenced by ecological risks, but also that it is more generally influenced by a sense of flux and uncertainty (McGuigan, 2005). The latter applies, too, on a personal level, where one's choice of career, partner and future, is – or at least is perceived to be – much more uncertain than used to be the case. Crucially, such a culture is a capitalist culture, McGuigan argues, and it contains cultural narratives of possibilities as well as uncertainties. McGuigan's last point is important, because it indicates how edgework and its narrative of personal growth are linked to capitalist entrepreneurship. As Lupton has mentioned (Lupton, 1999: 152), this link is visible among other things in business entrepreneurs – for example, the founder of Virgin, Sir Richard Branson – who become modern media icons embodying precisely both entrepreneurialism and adventurism. More generally, the edgework narrative of self-realization and growth has been taken and used in such sectors as business psychology, managerial science and coaching. In such a narrative, the entrepreneur is one who is able to shed conventional thinking and routine patterns of action and to invent. According to this same narrative, in business adventures one also is on the brink, close to the abyss, and, in order to survive, determination, stamina and cool decision making are needed – exactly as they are needed when, say, climbing Everest.

Practices such as mountain climbing and other forms of edgework may therefore be seen as part of a greater cultural narrative that glorifies risk taking, which also takes the form of entrepreneurialism and individual adventurism. Governmentality writers such as O'Malley and, above all, Baker and Simon have argued this most persuasively, Baker and Simon when talking about modern society embracing risk (Baker and Simon, 2002), and O'Malley when identifying a more entrepreneurial culture (O'Malley, 2003; 2004). One might also draw on Douglas, who says that contemporary society has become more entrepreneurial, meaning that the past is no longer seen as a guide for the future and that the significance of individual decision making is emphasized.

I have just taken some theoretical steps from edgework to individualization to capitalism and entrepreneurship. In order to go full circle, it is necessary to revise the starting point, namely edgework. Placing mountain climbing and other forms of voluntary risk taking in this greater context of risk, capitalism and entrepreneurialism means that Lyng's theoretical explanation for why edgework is becoming more widespread needs to be revised. As has been mentioned, Lyng originally interpreted edgework as a need to place oneself in situations where individual skills were crucial, or where narratives emphasizing individual skills could be plausibly constructed. That need was due to the alienating nature of life in modern society, where one's sense of one's own skills often disappears from view. However, Lyng himself has in later works acknowledged that voluntary risk taking might not only be a consequence of loss of self. Instead, voluntary risk taking is a practice that results from living in a society where the future is more open, and where individual management of risk and uncertainty, including taking chances, is encouraged and even glorified. This means, says Lyng, that there is a 'basic consistency or even a degree of synergy between edgework practices and the institutional order of the "second modernity"' (Lyng, 2005: 7). Lyng moreover links edgework not only to Beck's notion of the risk society, but also to the move from risk to uncertainty described by the governmentality tradition:

With the ascendancy of 'neoliberal' or 'post-Keynesian' political–economic policies in these societies . . . , the responsibility
for risks has been increasingly directed away from organizations and collectivities and displaced on to individuals. As
Jonathan Simon (this volume) points out, edgework and
centre work begin to blur in this context. (Lyng, 2005: 8)

Lyng here makes a crucial amendment to his notion of
edgework. He still focuses on voluntary risk taking, but he
acknowledges that such activities no longer take place only
at the margins of society; edgework is also becoming 'centre-
work'. The abnormal is perhaps in some places becoming
normal. Acknowledging this enables Lyng to see risk-taking
practices such as financial trading or gambling as edgework
(see Zaloom, 2006; Zwick, 2005). Lyng was originally reluc-
tant to define these practices as edgework, no doubt because
practices such as financial trading are very much at the centre
of capitalist society, which was precisely what he saw edge-
workers trying to avoid.

As for gambling, Lyng originally saw it as a game of pure
chance in which individual skills could only be expressed
with difficulty. Reith, in a fascinating study on gambling, has
shown that this need not be the case (Reith, 1999). Gamblers,
she shows, often try to construct accounts of their own gambling in which the outcome is not reduced to mere probability
distributions. Instead they create accounts of their own skill,
luck and ability to keep their cool. Reith explains this as a
need for re-enchantment. Knowledge about probability and
randomness is widespread in today's society. Randomness
does not merely take away responsibility and the importance
of individual action, but also takes away the magic, so to
speak. By constructing accounts of gambling in which the
individual takes action, seeks luck and awaits the unexplain-
able wonder, gamblers infuse empty and impersonal randomness with personal meaning. Reith does not stop, however, at
this idea of a need for re-enchantment. Just like Lyng in his
later works, she sees a connection between gambling, risk and
knowledge about probability. What unites them, above all, is
a culturally ingrained world view that emphasizes chance and
a more open future, a cultural world view which subsequently

valorizes entrepreneurialism and individualism. Or in slightly different terms – something which above all Reith's account shows – what is being valorized is above all the notion of individual control through actions and decision making. Whether climbing mountains, investing in stocks, taking up insurance policies, deciding when to hold playing cards or successfully starting up a business, it is the capability to foresee and steer through the many uncertainties and risks such activities entail that is being valorized.

A present future

I now wish to outline theoretically the contours of this cultural narrative of the risk society. It is a cultural narrative of risk in which the future is uncertain and unpredictable. The cultural narrative allows the uncertain future to assume different guises, however. It might be a future where the personal ability to steer through unknowns will be economically rewarded. It might be an uncertain future that is no longer controllable by the risk-reducing institutions and practices of the first modernity. And it might be an uncertain future with which one can play, or which creates a need for forms of play – gambling and other activities – that allow at least the illusion that one's own actions can influence the future. These three accounts of a more uncertain future loosely refer to governmentality, reflexive modernization and edgework. Douglas is missing here, but as mentioned above, one could use the grid-group model to interpret this cultural narrative as individualistic and entrepreneurial. In any case, to include Douglas's description of entrepreneurialism only serves to underline the central point: we are dealing with a cultural narrative in which a more open and more uncertain future features prominently.

Towards the end of chapter 2, I mentioned that the future has become an extended present; actual problems extend into the future and future problems loom over the present. For example, there is a grey area between total scientific knowledge and total ignorance, which consists of knowledge about possibilities and hence the future; scientific knowledge about possible risks means that there is enough knowledge about the future to make present decisions difficult and risky – if no such knowledge existed about the future, there would be less of a problem. In this and other ways, the future attains a much more marked 'present presence'. But based on what has been discussed so far, it must be added that this should not be understood only in a negative sense. The future may also open up in a positive sense, so that decisions, investments, strategies, gambling and simple daredevilry may be rewarded, making risk taking desirable. Echoing Pat O'Malley's description of neoliberal entrepreneurialism, Nowotny, Scott and Gibbons very much emphasize this in their description of what they call a mode-2 society, arguing that the present presence of the future is not due only to looming risks or scientific uncertainty:

> In a deeper sociological sense the key change is not so much the empirical fact that new kinds of risk are being created (although there are novel risks dramatically exemplified by the spread of the radioactive clouds produced by the accident at the Chernobyl nuclear power plant, unhindered across national boundaries in Europe. Rather, at the turn of the twenty-first century both individuals and societies have come to understand themselves and to define many of their problems in terms of the technologies and semantics of risk . . . It is important to recognize that the new uncertainties in knowledge production are not simply a result of the intensification of the old Socratic maxim that 'to know more is to know what we don't know'; nor is their cause technological and economic globalization. Rather, on a historically unprecedented scale, both science and society have opted for the production of the New in an open process of moving towards a plurality of unknown futures. (Nowotny, Scott and Gibbons, 2001: 34–5)

This rather grand statement can be taken to mean many things (perhaps too many), but it does capture a fundamental cultural change in thinking about and acting on the future, and it drives home the point about the future's 'present presence'.

Also, the statement points to how the cultural change extends way beyond culture per se – into the economy, for example. Nowotny, Scott and Gibbons point to such things as more financial investment in highly uncertain business ventures (for instance, in the biotechnology industry) that can only possibly yield rewards in the long term; and they point, also, to new types of financial speculation, for example in financial derivatives. What such examples have in common is that the investment is really in the uncertain future. The future itself almost becomes the product and, as such, it attains the aforementioned 'present presence'. One illustration of this could be a new industry that has emerged around stem-cell technology. Parents about to have children are offered to have blood from the umbilical cord collected, frozen and stored in special 'banks' so that the blood can be used to extract stem cells later in the child's life. The point is that stem-cell technology could potentially be used in the future against a series of pernicious diseases. This industry thus handsomely illustrates the future's present presence. Parents buying the product are literally banking on technological progress in the future. The precise benefits cannot be specified. What is offered is a highly uncertain insurance against the risk of diseases that might afflict the child (at a later stage, when the child has become an adult). The decision, however, has to be taken now. The child's future is very much present for the parents. Setting up an account at an umbilical cord blood bank is an option (Lind and Arnoldi, 2006); one acquires a possible insurance against possible future ills. It is illustrative of a culture where the future and future dangers are anticipated well in advance and where such anticipated future dangers gain economic significance.

Niklas Luhmann has presented arguably the most advanced theoretical analysis of the role of time and the future in contemporary culture. Modern society, Luhmann argues, has developed a conception of the future that means that more contingency or complexity can be observed. By observing complexity, Luhmann above all means that actions are attributed to more, and to a more diverse range of, future consequences (Luhmann, 1993: 46). The predominant notion of causation in contemporary knowledge and also culture more generally is one in which causal relations are seen as contingent and unpredictable (Luhmann, 1997: 1011).

Every attempt to specify causalities engenders ever greater difficulties. What will happen never depends on a single event. It is always a concatenation of circumstances, so that uncertainty multiplies in proportion to the rigour of the analysis. Within the horizon of the past one at least knows what has happened, even if causal relations remain unclear. (Luhmann, 1993: 41)

Luhmann's system theoretic notion of complexity, on which his arguments about time, risk and causation rest, is hard to fathom, perhaps because it is at bottom a paradox. Any system (person, group, organization or society) is faced with complexity, in the sense that a wide range of future events could potentially spring from the present. No system can ignore this array of possibilities, incomprehensible or even scary as they may be. Decisions need to be made. Systems are therefore forced to make decisions based on expectations about their consequences, even if an overview of these consequences is hard to obtain. 'Expectation' is the term Luhmann uses, but it is slightly misleading, as he means above all knowledge (Luhmann, 1995: 328) and the schemata embedded in knowledge (Luhmann, 2000: 110) – for instance, scientific knowledge about causation.

Luhmann's point in all this is that systems faced with complexity are forced to form more fluid schemata that can take the multitude of possibilities into account (Luhmann, 1995: 320). Yet – and here Luhmann deliberately constructs a paradox – by taking these many possibilities into account, the future is experienced as even more complex. The complexity that Luhmann describes lies in the eye of the beholder, or, in sociological terms, is constructed. More complex expectations (knowledge) about the future create an ability to take more complexity into account. This construction is a necessity, however. Modern society is forced to create forms of knowledge that can account for complexity because it is faced with more complexity. If one were to phrase this using the vocabulary of Michel Callon (see chapter 4), one would say that the overflows of hot translations force through broader frames that render more future possibilities possible.

Luhmann's description of changing temporal and causal schemata is of course a description of a cultural change.

Culturally ingrained schemata with which things in the world are apprehended, communicated about and acted upon have changed; they have, as Luhmann puts it, been modalized (Luhmann, 1995: 320; 2000: 83), that is, become more plastic, so that more things, good or bad, can be expected as a possibility. Enter not only risks, but also entrepreneurial opportunities.

Calculating the risks, not knowing the odds

The future, I have argued, looms over the present. It is more unpredictable and at the same time more present, in the sense that the future must be decided upon and speculated in, chances taken, dangers avoided and so on. If we turn to the analytical distinction between risk and uncertainty, then these are examples of future uncertainty. But the future may also be more present in the form of calculable risk. Nowotny, Scott and Gibbons show that another way in which the future comes to be more present is through the creation of new techniques for knowing or forming expectations about the future. Prominent among these techniques are various forms of probability calculation, something I touched on in chapter 5 when I discussed the performative power of modern science. Probability and probabilistic risks calculus are increasingly used in different sectors of modern society, including, of course, the insurance and finance industries.

Governmentality scholars such as Ericsson and Doyle have criticized Beck for emphasizing uncertainty and disregarding risks, that is, claiming that insurance against future dangers is becoming more problematic (Ericson and Doyle, 2004a). Ericson and Doyle point out that insurance today is a business more widespread and more in use than ever before; in the risk society there is not less insurance but more. Importantly, Ericson and Doyle also show that the success of insurance should not be interpreted as the triumph of risk over uncertainty in the sense that the probability of all future dangers can be calculated. Although insurance is built on probability calculations, insurance as a business involves a considerable degree of uncertainty. Often insurers do not quite know the odds, so they take chances (Ericson and Doyle, 2004b: 5–8; Ericson, Doyle and Barry, 2003: 9). Put differently, insurance underwriting is not about sure bets but about being entrepreneurial, overcoming uncertainty.

Such descriptions indicate that an increased prevalence of both risk and uncertainty exists in the risk society. There are more probabilistic risk calculations – the insurance industry, for instance, profits both from more sophisticated computer technology and more sophisticated databases and mathematical models. But there is also more uncertainty, which means more business opportunities. In the case of insurance, this is because more products are being created, and in the case of private insurance the downscaling of state social and health insurance for political reasons has created new markets for private insurance products.

The insurance industry clearly finds itself challenged by new risks emerging in the risk society. After the 9/11 attack, private insurers in the United States incurred very big losses and were suddenly facing new threats that they had not hitherto anticipated (Ericson and Doyle, 2004a). One response was to cancel existing contracts, to impose strict new terms on new contracts and to exercise extreme caution before underwriting risks linked to terrorism. Also, because reinsurers often backed out, federal government support was needed to help primary insurers. The end result was that the insurance industry did not altogether shy away from these new risk scenarios; rather, insurance companies have created advanced new models in an effort to reduce some of the vast uncertainty to calculable risk (Ericson and Doyle, 2004a). A somewhat similar scenario can be found with regard to global warming. In particular the reinsurers – the companies that insure the insurance companies – have responded with great concern to global warming and the changing weather patterns caused by it. By the early 1990s reinsurers had already noted an increase in insurance claims after floods and hurricanes, and they connected this increase to global warming. In response they have done some lobbying, trying to convince policymakers to reduce carbon dioxide emissions. The main response of the insurance industry has, however, been to increase premiums and to reduce in other ways their risk exposure and develop advanced new models of risk calculation (Paterson, 2001).

Insurers and reinsurers have also been able to offload some of their exposure to low probability–high consequence risks by selling the risks to investors on the financial markets. Such contracts, so-called catastrophe bonds (cat-bonds), stipulate that the holder (buyer) is entitled to a specified payment after a specified time, should no disasters (e.g. hurricanes) occur. In the case of a disaster, the holder loses this right. Although risky for obvious reasons, cat-bonds offer a high potential yield and are therefore attractive for risk-seeking investors. As Bougen points out, such contracts further blur the boundaries between finance and insurance (Bougen, 2003). They show both the problems that the insurance industry faces with low probability–high consequence risks and one possible solution. And, perhaps above all, such contracts show how, in a contemporary capitalist society, uncertainties and risk are parlayed into potential profits for speculators seeking risks. This dynamic arguably applies not only to willing financial players but also to the insurance industry itself. Even though some insurance underwriting might simply represent a gamble because the potential dangers can be calculated (making them uncertainties rather than risks), insurers might still opt to take that gamble. Ericsson and Doyle quote a reinsurance executive delivering a conference speech after 9/11:

> We love ambiguity. We know how to handle uncertainty. And I think that we know it much better than the average consumer or the buyer of our products. Risk has always two dimensions. It is a threat, a peril, but it also contains the aspect of opportunity. And the art is to balance these two, threat and opportunity, in a smart and conscious way. (Anonymous, quoted in Ericson and Doyle, 2004a: 148)

These two dimensions of risk and uncertainty mean that the risk society is not a society where either risk or uncertainty dominates. Instead, it is a society where there is more of both risk *and* uncertainty. Potential new dangers, such as the risk of global terror, are met with a mixture of risk calculus and capitalist entrepreneurialism.

The same mix of risk and entrepreneurial uncertainty can be found in finance. In chapter 5, I mentioned the so-called derivatives markets. Derivatives trading can be a way for investors to shield themselves from the risks of investments, but these markets also allow for much more speculation. This is because it is cheaper to buy the risk of owning securities than to buy the actual securities. In effect, being able to buy more risk obviously also means exposing oneself to more risk, yet the practice is also attractive because it means the possibility of a bigger profit.

The creation of derivatives markets is almost solely a result of the invention of new advanced probabilistic techniques (MacKenzie and Millo, 2003). That is risk, but the creation of such markets has at the same time allowed for new and highly speculative forms of finance – what has been called 'casino capitalism' (Comaroff and Comaroff, 2000). That is uncertainty – so just as with the insurance industry, we find here a mix of risk and uncertainty, risk reduction and risk taking.

I started this section by mentioning the debates between Beck and Ericsson and Doyle regarding risk, uncertainty and insurance, and I will end it with the same. Beck has often argued that insurance, which he sees as a risk-management institution of the first modernity, is struggling to cope with low probability–high consequence risks. Beck has suggested that new low probability–high consequence risks often cannot be insured at all, making insurability a handy litmus test for establishing which risks are new and which belong to the first modernity. Ericsson and Doyle argue that this is not the case (Ericson and Doyle, 2004a). Risks such as those of terrorist attacks or nuclear accidents are, and always have been for that matter, insurable. Ericsson and Doyle grant Beck that low probability–high consequence risks to some extent may escape calculability, but insurance is not only about calculating risk; it is also about taking chances. Beck for his part acknowledges that the sharp distinction between insurable and uninsurable was a mistake. What is observable, however – and also in Ericsson's and Doyle's studies, he argues – is a radical reconfiguration of private insurance. When it comes to 'new' risks, insurability is often contingent on support from the state, which then effectively acts as reinsurer.

Furthermore, private insurance companies are forced to stipulate a range of exceptions from liability in order to shield themselves from eventualities that are bigger than their claims-paying capacities. Beck concludes that *private* insurance is in a state of crisis. In extreme cases, it is viable only if backed by government; and this crisis, although not as self-evident as he once argued, is an indicator of there being risks of a new kind.

An example of this is wind-storm insurance in Florida, where insurance companies have radically raised premiums and refused to renew several hundred thousand insurance policies against hurricane damage. In a single step, one company abandoned 226,000 customers, one-third of its client base in Florida (*The Economist*, 11 August 2007: 38). The many people who find themselves unable to get coverage have been helped by a new insurance company, Citizens Property Insurance, financed by the state of Florida. However, the risk exposure is high for the state, too, so the governor of Florida has called for a federal scheme in order to spread the risk.

The governmentality tradition on the other hand agrees that there is more incalculable uncertainty (Beck is chastised for not using this more fitting term for incalculable risks) but focuses much more on relations between uncertainty and entrepreneurialism. When it comes to insurance and also finance, the focus of the governmentality tradition on this relationship offers a crucial insight, and arguably one that Beck fails to account for: new uncertainties both have arisen from and have themselves created a new economic scenario in which not only dangers but also economic opportunities exist – at least for some. Hence a risk-seeking financial system seems to be one social institution that in an uncertain world actually prevails rather than being thrown into a state of crisis.

Risk and the burden of responsibility

No matter in which form the open future looms over the present, it contains a hidden imperative to act, to decide.

There is a strong element of individualization inherent in the confrontation with risk and an open future, an individualization that manifests itself in several ways. One way is that mistrust in expertise and conflicting expert opinions force the layperson to make individual choices (Beck, 2007: 107). A second way involves individual risk taking as leisure, increasingly consumed as pre-packaged objects of consumption, for example a pre-packaged trip to Mount Everest. Such risk taking is initiated in order to feel individual, to feel that one's own actions matter. A third way is the many forms of insurance that are commercially available, for instance, health insurance, where more and more data and better actuarial knowledge allow health insurance companies to offer almost tailor-made insurance polices to individual customers – based, of course, on the risk profile of each customer (Ericson, Doyle and Barry, 2003). A fourth way, in many respects opposed to the first, is through various policies and expert practices wherein individuals are actively encouraged to become more self-reliant or to take their own decisions. The medical routines for hormone replacement therapy, described in chapter 5, serve as an example, but the fourth way more generally takes place through information campaigns and other means of creating public awareness about various risks (the risks of smoking being an obvious example). Fifth, economic risk taking is also encouraged by government – for instance, through the sort of pension schemes common in the United States, where each member has to make financial investments (Simon, 2004: 179).

What unites all these very different roles played by risk, and also what gives risk its individualizing power, is that risk creates and distributes responsibility (Baker, 2004). Once we know that something is risky, we are confronted with an unspoken imperative to take action either collectively or privately. As for the social distribution of risks (a specific form of not goods but 'bads'), both Beck and the governmentality scholars have shown that a situation has developed where more of this responsibility is now falling to the individual. For the governmentality scholars, this trend is part of a general cultural and political change in society, in which self-reliance and individual risk management are valorized. Included in this valorization of individual risk management is not only risk minimization, but also risk *taking*, such as extreme sports or financial speculation. No doubt these forms of risk taking are valorized because they fit well into a cultural and governmental narrative which valorizes being capable of independent risk management, being mentally strong enough to withstand risk, and daring to take risks and hence accomplish.

The cultural or governmental changes identified are not primarily movements from less risk taking to more risk taking (or vice versa) but above all changes as to which *forms* of risk avoidance and risk taking are valorized and which not. As an example, for an ordinary person to invest in the market was for a long time seen as much too risky – even immoral. After the Great Depression of the 1930s, the US government even imposed draconian measures to reduce speculation in stock exchanges because the practice was seen as too risky and too irresponsible. But things have changed. As mentioned above, retirement schemes now involve individual investment. O'Malley, in a genealogy of uncertainty, shows that governments and law courts have used varying distinctions among insurance, gambling and speculation, attaching very different moral connotations to each of these, if not outright banning some of them (O'Malley, 2004). The point is that definitions of which actions are moral entrepreneurialism and which immoral gambling and speculation have changed markedly over time. For example, it was not until the 1870s that life insurance in the United States came to be seen as morally acceptable, rather than immoral. Similarly, the development of derivatives markets was delayed in many countries because of legal frameworks that defined, and forbade, such forms of speculation as gambling (Leslie and Wyatt, 1992: 88). Since the 1970s this has changed through a process in which, initially, new expert economic discourse had to be constructed. The new discourse defined such practices as speculation, thereby allowing for the legislation to be altered (O'Malley, 2003).

On the other hand, smoking or other activities related to unhealthy lifestyles are increasingly condemned because they are too risky. Risks are always part of moral systems in which some forms of risk taking are deemed acceptable while others are not. Similarly, but on a much smaller scale, the moral narrative of edgework is constantly renegotiated. Mountain climbing and Everest can once again provide a specific example in the dramatic events of 1996. That year, the American socialite (itself a derogatory term in this context) Sandy Hill Pittman attracted much criticism after she survived the storm that killed Green Boots, as well as several people in her climbing party, including one of the guides. She attracted bad press essentially because her attempt to climb Everest came to be seen as something approaching tourism rather than real, 'authentic', adventure. Because a rich American woman survived an attempt to climb Everest while a guide in her service died, the edgework narrative of individual skills as being key to survival and personal self-realization arguably came under threat and had to be reconstructed and reinforced by moral condemnation.

Summary

This chapter has identified a range of cultural practices, discourses and schemata that have become predominant in, and characterize, the risk society. I have written about very different things – mountain climbing, gambling, stem cells, insurance and finance – but at least three things bind them all together. First, these practices, discourses and schemata hinge on a conception of the future as more open, more contingent and yet also more present. This open future takes multiple forms, I have argued, because it contains both possible dangers and opportunities, and it looms more over the present both in the form of calculable risk and incalculable uncertainty. Second, these cultural changes are also political, economic and governmental. They belong to new forms of government and economic life, with new forms of economic action and consumption and new distributions of responsibility between the state and the individual. Third, I have suggested that the cultural changes in many ways accentuate the individual, both in terms of responsibilities and possibilities. The movements towards advanced liberalism have been driven by a rethinking of risk and uncertainty. These changes have led to new distributions of responsibility between the individual and the state, have allowed for financial markets and private insurance companies to play more significant roles in society, and have generally idealized and valorized ideas of entrepreneurship and individual control. I return to the relations between risk, individualization and responsibilization in the next chapter.

One must, however, be careful before rushing to the conclusion that there is now less state and more market or individualism, or less risk and more uncertainty. As we shall see in the next chapter, the state has taken on new responsibilities, above all as a provider of security against (the risk of) terrorism. As the example of hurricane insurance in Florida shows, individual states have also been forced to take on other responsibilities And the acknowledgement that some things might be uncertain and not calculable has led to regulation based on precaution, in which the nation states (and supranational institutions and regimes) play a key role as regulators.

The more open and more present future, along with the hidden imperative to act and decide individually, is no doubt a psychological and emotional burden for many people. There is less certainty and there are more choices to be made – and even when individuals do take decisions, they may feel that such decisions have no effect in a world where contingency rules. But such an open future with all its possible dangers also leads to new forms of play and leisure. Perhaps the description here, and the theory of edgework more generally because of its basis in a notion of alienation, do not show clearly enough the pleasures sought by taking risks. There is a strong element of hedonism in modern culture (Featherstone, 1991), created no doubt by the fact that large groups of affluent middle-class individuals have relatively large amounts of money and time – the latter both in terms of free time and long periods in their lives when it is culturally acceptable to be young and to experiment. A good deal of this spare time and experimenting is consumed by various forms of mild risk taking, such as extreme sports, drug taking, sexual experimentation and so on (see Lupton, 1999: 163–71). This is not so much risk taking as it is thrill seeking, seeking a kick, getting the adrenaline flowing in the secure knowledge that actually there is little real danger. Bungee jumping would be an example. One should therefore be careful seeing all such practices as edgework in the classical sense (Seigneur, 2006). But, nevertheless, these practices also belong in a cultural narrative which valorizes adventure, dynamism and taking chances.

And on a final note, the neoliberal discourse of entrepreneurship is perhaps a very gendered discourse, celebrating and reinstating traditional male characteristics of adventurousness, risk taking and courage. The concept of risk is arguably a vehicle for gender politics in this regard. That said, female versions are also played out, in the business world also, where, for example, the female potential for entrepreneurship is being constructed in business literature (Bröckling, 2005).

9
Risk, politics and government

The power of defining risk

It has been lurking just under the surface all the time, and now, finally, it is to be dealt with explicitly: risks are political. Indeed, one of the reasons why risk is such an important part of contemporary society is the political significance of risks. Discussions of which risks are worst and what should be done about them are obviously political discussions. Worries about risks, and calls for regulation and protective measures, create whole new areas of responsibility for government. Perhaps for this reason, new political ideologies and techniques of government have emerged that focus much less on the abolishment of risk and more on risk prevention and risk management, and place more responsibility on the shoulders of each single individual. These last remarks also show that politics and risks not only have to do with how to govern, regulate, pool and distribute risks. Risk simultaneously becomes a tool for governing, for creating responsibility for the individual citizen also, and for creating new areas of government intervention and new techniques for intervention.

This chapter will deal with both politics *and* government and, furthermore, it will deal with both government *of* risk and government *with* (concepts of) risk. Government of risk relates closely to political struggles over how risks should be managed and distributed. Government with risk relates to the ways in which concepts of risk are being constructed in scientific and political thought and subsequently used in various forms of government, including penal systems, social insurance, health systems and other institutions.

With uncertainties surrounding the use of new technologies and public concerns about the ensuing risks, a new political situation emerges. Public debates start to rage and critical questions are put forward, both to scientists and to politicians. This creates not only a range of new burdens and responsibilities for political decision makers and governments, but also a whole new dynamic of politics. In the 1970s, in most Western countries, green issues became major political issues, giving rise to the emergence of green parties in most of the countries in question. With some exceptions, for example Germany and currently Switzerland, these parties have played relatively minor roles in most countries. One major reason is no doubt that existing political parties quickly responded by incorporating environmental issues into their own political programmes. But at the same time, even though green parties have gained little ground in parliaments, green issues have fostered a range of interest groups, neighbourhood alliances, lobby groups and so on, that promote environmental issues, protest against environmental degradation or otherwise seek to promote risk reduction or regulation. That is, much of environmental politics is taking place outside the established political institutions, and green issues have invigorated civil involvement in politics. I showed in chapter 4 how environmental issues have dragged science into the political fray – for example when scientists are questioned by a sceptical, perhaps even distrustful, public, or when scientists are enlisted by interest groups or themselves enter debates. But the same issues have also to some extent dragged politics away from the traditional political institutions.

Beck uses the term 'sub-politics' to denote the disconnection of politics from government (Beck, 2007: 178), something that I touched upon above, namely that a range of political issues are, if not decided, then at least framed outside the parliaments and governments of nation states. 'Sub-politics' hence means new ways of seeking influence, new forums for politics – for example, through interest groups, consumer boycotts, local citizens' groups and so on (Holzer and Sørensen, 2003). Some have also argued that environmental interest groups and other political movements based on concerns about risks are examples of identity politics, meaning that people do not so much unite around a political agenda as around a more deep-seated and shared sense of being disenfranchised or marginalized – in the case of risk perhaps as much from science and knowledge as from influences on political decision making (see, e.g., Tesh, 2000: 102).

Concerns about risk instigate public discussion and public activity (Beck and Grande, 2004: 315). Such public debates often occur by means of the mass media (see chapter 7). They are laden with different symbols and connotations. For example, different meanings ascribed to nature (see chapter 4) are being used rhetorically to promote specific political interests. This is arguably one of the defining characteristics of risks politics: the political struggles are not merely over how to distribute risk and responsibility – that is, debates over who should be exposed to what and to what degree, and who is responsible. Instead, they are as much over the definition of what constitutes the most pressing risks – that is, they are definitional struggles over what is risky as much as they are struggles over the distribution and management of risk per se. Risks themselves – that is, the social construction of risks and not only their distribution – are political.

It follows that great political power lies in being able to define what is risky (Beck, 2007: 70). This is why science, which has suddenly been granted a new kind of influence, has become democratically important, as we saw in chapter 5. More generally, being able to shape public perceptions of risk – having a voice and imposing one's values, and one's framings, on the public debate – equals political power. Often, this means having access to the mass media, which, we saw in chapter 6, serve as important stations in the social amplification processes.

The great merit of a social constructionist approach to risks is the insight that defining, or constructing, risks equals power. There is political power in playing a leading role in social amplification processes, and political actors seek to shape such amplification processes to maintain their interests.

Social constructionist studies of risk do not merely study the, to some extent arbitrary, formations of public risk perceptions – they also implicitly ask: who benefits? In the social amplification processes power structures are maintained and 'others' are excluded (Douglas, 1992).

The notion of sub-politics is often used to argue how grassroot or other forms of 'politics from below' are important in political processes involving risk, even providing the impetus to regulate risks. However, recent developments might be reason to question this. At least in the case of global warming, it seems as if the response comes from high politics, perhaps in conjunction with other social elites. One thing is at least certain, namely that much of risk politics and government happens in various transnational and supranational institutions. This at least is sub-politics in another form.

Transnational risk regulation

Risks raise important political questions about trust and accountability. As above all Anthony Giddens has repeatedly argued, trust, or the lack thereof, is a crucial element in risks politics and also in modern society in general. The public may not so much demand that the scientific basis for risks regulation is sound as they may demand that the decision-making processes of government bodies are transparent and accountable. Brian Wynne (Wynne, 1996: 57–58) has pointed out that laypeople take stock not of the scientists but of the regulatory bodies before deciding whether or not technologies can be trusted. This attention to regulatory bodies is based on the assumption that the scientific uncertainties surrounding the issues are so great that understanding the science is of limited value, besides being fraught with difficulties. Instead, and quite rationally so, the public looks to the institutions and procedures that regulate risk: Do they show willingness to change positions when new evidence surfaces? Do they have transparent procedures? In short, are they trustworthy and accountable? Such concerns and demands show just how central questions about democratic and legal accountability are to problems of risk. Sound democratic risks regulation may not so much hinge on public understanding of science as on accountable and transparent risks regulation.

However, accountability is something that is hampered by the very nature of risks. The transnational nature of risk, for example, means that legal accountability is difficult because the polluter might be in another country, or because it is simply impossible to establish who the culprits are. There is often 'a *spatial mismatch* between national territories of governmental responsibility and transboundary pathways of (potential) harm' (Mason, 2005: 2, emphasis in original). The scientific uncertainties regarding many risks also mean that there are no clearly defined premises on which political decision making can proceed. In a similar vein, nation states are trying to provide security with a conventional security apparatus of police, army, and (although these no doubt defy national conventions) intelligence services in the face of new terrorist threats that defy most conventional concepts of enemy combatants. This poses a series of challenges for political institutions and decision makers.

New supra- and transnational governance regimes have attained an increasingly important role as risks increasingly transcend national boundaries. As well, this evolving role may be seen as a form of subpoliticization, because here, too, political activities are taking place outside the typical political institutions of national parliaments and governments. The nature of these new actors and institutions is very heterogeneous, ranging from supranational government institutions such as the Organization for Economic Cooperation and Development or the World Trade Organization (Tait and Bruce, 2001), to more informal government regimes such as the Commission on Plant Genetic Resources, to international non-governmental organizations. The political arenas are in other words moving both upwards (supranational) and sideways (to non-governmental organizations and public–private partnerships).

The notion of risk regulation regimes is often used in studies of (above all transnational) risk regulation (e.g. Hood, Rothstein and Baldwin, 2004). The term is used for several reasons. One is that risk regulation is an unruly affair, which not only comprises a single set of rules laid out by one decision-making political institution, but also comprises many overlapping rules, some informal, some formal, and a set of actors and decision makers on different levels and with different functions. Regime analysis attempts to capture this in its totality. Another reason is that transnational regulatory agreements and practices vastly transcend the institutional boundaries of the nation states, but are nevertheless systemic and functional. Regimes (at least transnational regimes) are in this sense sub-political because they are systems of governance that extend and override the sovereignty and the political institutions of nation states (Grande and Pauly, 2005).

Cosmopolitanism

Transnational regimes of risk regulation are one example of what Ulrich Beck calls the cosmopolitan condition of contemporary society. Cosmopolitanism is an old concept, denoting a way of thinking about the world as a single society, or at least thinking beyond single nation states. In Beck's work, cosmopolitanism means forms of thought and (inter)action that go beyond the national but do not mean the abolishment of, or polar opposite to, the national and nation states. Yet the national and nation states are supplemented by transnational and global social and cultural formations, one example being the above mentioned risk regulation regimes. This does not lead to global unity and, to repeat, it does not mean the abolishment of nation states. For example, nation states continue to wield considerable power in, and over, supranational risk regulation regimes (Fisher, 2003). Beck therefore seeks to place the notion of cosmopolitanism in between the poles of nationalism and globalism. Cosmopolitanism entails a 'both and' – both nationalism and globalism – and it therefore adequately describes the complex transnational risk regimes that need not be truly global and that do not lead to abolishing nation states.

Cosmopolitanism has usually been a normative and philosophical idea. Traditionally it has meant a commitment to being a world citizen – a willingness to cast aside nationality, ethnicity, religion and other ideas of belonging. Beck acknowledges this normative tradition, but the reason for his interest is that he believes that the world itself has become cosmopolitan (Beck, 2004: 8). This is real, or what he sometimes calls banal, cosmopolitanization, that is, a social process whereby the interdependencies between nation states are increasing dramatically. Cosmopolitanization happens when people, products, ideas and information increasingly cross geographical boundaries and when events and problems evoke in people's minds an imagining and sense of solidarity that goes beyond the confines of the national. Risks play no small part in this. Beck talks of four different axes of conflict that create interdependency crises: ecological risks, financial risks, terror risks and, finally, moral interdependency crises caused by the proliferation of human rights (Beck and Znaider, 2006: 11). These problems trigger public awareness that goes beyond the national, that is, they create a transnational risk community (Beck and Znaider, 2006: 11). They also, we saw above, trigger transnational political cooperation of the type previously described.

What seems most important to Beck in this regard is the subpoliticization that he has increasingly come to view as cosmopolitan. Social movements are increasingly transnational, and political debates are increasingly about matters that have global implications. Even anti-globalization movements, he notes, are cosmopolitan, because they are building on transnational cooperation. It is worth mentioning, by the way, that Beck sees cosmopolitanization as being different from globalization, which he sees as being mainly economic and as a process that is external to (although it affects) the individual. In contrast, Beck sees cosmopolitanization as being internally driven. It starts with a subjective experience of interdependency.

As described earlier, Beck has throughout his work emphasized that the risk society is not necessarily a more dangerous society, but rather one in which risks are increasingly raised as concerns and problems in public and political debates. As Mason eloquently shows, concerns about accountability play a huge part in this because one central role of the public sphere is to hold to account those responsible. Mason quotes Dewey, arguing that Dewey's classical description of the problem of the public sphere is more important than ever before:

An inchoate public is capable of organization only when indirect consequences are perceived, and when it is possible to project agencies which order their occurrence. At present, many consequences are felt rather than perceived, they are suffered, but they cannot be said to be known, for they are not, by those who experience them, referred to their origins. (Dewey quoted in Mason, 2005: 170–1).

Dewey shows that it is difficult to maintain a democratic public sphere when responsibility is disorganized and when it escapes national political structures. But an optimistic interpretation of the quotation would also emphasize the potential inherent in this – the potential of people trying to seek out the 'agencies who order their occurrence' (something that the existence of transnational risk regulation regimes makes easier), in the process forming a cosmopolitan public sphere. One might then counter such optimistic accounts by pointing to the fact that public discussions about risk concern disagreement about risks as much as who is accountable – something that we saw in chapter 6. However, the public sphere is not supposed to foster agreement but only foster debates. And that certainly seems to be happening.

Terror, war and risk

There is no need to state that 9/11 marked a point in history after which global terror assumed a very prominent position in the political agenda. Indeed, there might even be a tendency today to see security rather than welfare as the most pressing responsibility of governments (Mythen and Walklate, 2005). Attempts to provide security for citizens have created a range of new government initiatives around the world, in many cases creating tensions between civil and human rights and ideas of security. People are being abducted, held without trial and tortured, all in the name of security and in blatant breach of human and legal rights. For example, the principle of habeas corpus, hitherto deeply rooted in the common law traditions of the United Kingdom and the United States, is being nullified. In the name of security, the Western world finds itself in a state of emergency on the basis of which democratic rights are nullified. Georgio Agamben is famous for a deliberate philosophical/historical analysis of what he calls states of exception, arguing that these states reduce people to bare life over which the sovereign power can then preside (Agamben, 1998). The most horrific example of this was the German concentration camps during the Holocaust, but the question Agamben poses is just how different, in principle if not in magnitude, Camp X-ray, secret interrogation camps around the world and the abolition of civil rights by so many governments really are.

Ulrich Beck was quick to include the risk of terror in his description of the world risk society, something that has drawn considerable criticism. One reason for this is that while the other potential dangers described by Beck are unintended side effects, terror is intended. Another reason is that some find Beck's response after 9/11 excessive, given that many terrorist acts had previously taken place and that in most Western countries the statistical likelihood of this particular danger has not increased significantly in the past decade. Yet Beck's point has always been that statistical likelihood matters less than the degree to which the risks are publicly anticipated and politically problematized. In that regard, of course, a sea change has occurred, not least because the mass media are being used strategically by terrorist organizations. I also mentioned in chapter 3 that modern terrorists use technology, albeit intentionally, and that they are global.

The risk of terror has certainly put security high not only on the political agenda but also on the agenda of the mass media, which of course serves only to enhance the political pressure. The media attention means that issues to do with social amplification of risks are relevant to the risk of terror, just as they are relevant to other risks. And while on the topic of social construction of risk, we should recognize that the risk of terror is of course used discursively and politically in the way described by Douglas. New divisions are created, coercion is practised and political interests are pursued through constructing a dangerous enemy. This is in stark contradiction to Beck's hope for a more cosmopolitan world order. The discursive construction of enemies as a political means is something that is increasingly studied by political scientists in the field of security studies. In regard to security studies, it is also worth mentioning that ecological problems and other types of risk are increasingly viewed by the same political scientists as also posing threats to the military and to the political security of states.

Clausewitz's old thesis that war is the continuation of politics by other means resonates strangely with a diagnosis by Martin Shaw of changes in contemporary warfare (Shaw, 2005). Shaw argues that wars undertaken by Western countries are increasingly risk-transfer wars. The traditional, 'industrial' war with thousands of soldiers being sent into battle is being replaced by technological forms of war, where the massive numbers of soldiers on the ground are replaced by long-range cruise missiles, unmanned drones and covert operations. These tactics reduce the risk of casualties (of servicemen and women), which in turn, and this is the real significance, reduces the political risks for political leaders. However, experience also shows that the risks are not reduced but rather transferred, most often to the civilian population in the country or area of conflict. Attempts to reduce political risks lead to increased risk of so-called collateral damage which means that civilians are being killed.

Security's coming before welfare and other types of government provision, and not least the many political initiatives to deliver security, have significant implications. As we shall see later, the emphasis on security has meant not only a departure from otherwise firmly established ideals of liberties and rights, but also heavy expenditure by governments who otherwise see themselves as neoliberal and fiscally conservative. This has been most clear in the case of the administration of President George W. Bush in the United States, which has drawn considerable criticism from its own ranks for creating 'big government' with ballooning public expenditures. This objection has been raised, by the way, not only in regard to security and anti-terrorism initiatives, but also in connection with aid programmes for the victims of Hurricane Katrina in the New Orleans area and initiatives to prevent similar disasters in the future. Risks, together with their actual catastrophic manifestations, change politics. Some of these government initiatives – especially some of the anti-terrorism measures – that go against the grain of liberalism also mark a departure from what governmentality theorists call 'government at a distance' (Rose, 1999: 49). Rather than subtly conducting conduct by creating specific subjectivities and so on, many security initiatives rely on much more explicit forms of power, for example the legally sanctioned use of torture when interrogating terror suspects. However, many of the measures remain categorizable as government at a distance. Chief among these is, of course, another form of power also analysed in detail by governmentality theorists, namely surveillance.

Crime and risks

Actuarial knowledge (statistical knowledge originally used in the insurance industry) about the risk of crime is increasingly used in technologies of government to manage and reduce crime. For example, statistical knowledge is used to identify city zones with high crime risks and to manage the built and social environment in such zones, so that crime is hindered or made more difficult. The paradigmatic symbol of much contemporary crime reduction technology, O'Malley remarks, is no longer the panopticon but the speed bump, that is, a technological installation that seeks to manage the behaviour of people not by curing pathologies but simply by making unwanted actions (speeding in this case) difficult (O'Malley, 1998b: xii). Obviously technologies can combine features related to both the speed bump and the panopticon, closed-circuit television (CCTV) surveillance being the best example (Yesil, 2006).

Surveillance technology is one of a series of measures through which urban areas with high crime risks are governed and changed. Urban spaces are increasingly designed to make criminal behaviour as difficult as possible. Street lighting is designed and arranged so that crime-risk zones are well lit and entrances to shop buildings are made visible from the street, while the less visible back of the buildings are highly secured, often with no or limited access. Such measures are taken not necessarily by central planners but rather by individual property developers and architects who use a battery of expert knowledge on crime risk and crime prevention, in some cases provided by police officers who act as consultants. This decentralized nature of planning and design is another reason why the notion of 'government at a distance' is a useful description. Power is being exercised neither directly nor by one central agent but by means of a body of knowledge about crime risks and a range of technologies which have been made available and which are used by various agents with the aim of altering the behaviour of criminal members of the public. This decentralized and distanced form of government also means that it is not absolute or total. Reluctance to make big investments in security technologies, such as CCTV, and many other factors means that there are often discrepancies and instances where the conduct of conduct fails (Parnaby, 2007). However, it is beyond doubt that the proliferation of these measures has great impact on the urban environment. It is, for example, easy to see how commercial areas such as shopping centres or malls have become more securitized, something that has put traditional public spaces at a disadvantage because people are attracted to areas with abundant and visible security measures. The distribution of safe areas versus risky ones, and hence centre versus margin in the urban environment is thus being altered.

In regard to sentencing, there has been talk of a 'new penology', which, it is argued, has emerged since the 1970s. The notion of a 'new penology' refers to a diverse set of changes in 'discourse, objectives and techniques' (Feeley and Simon, 1992: 449) in the penal system in which actuarial techniques feature heavily. The change is from an old penology which, among other things, was built on ideas of criminality being somatic. That is, old penology saw criminality as something that could be treated with correction and therapy, granting individual criminals the moral and psychological resources to change the course of their life and rehabilitate. In contrast, the new penology does not seek to eliminate the underlying causes but rather to manage populations on the basis of statistical data about the types of criminal that pose the highest risks and the kinds of environment that have the highest likelihood of triggering criminal behaviour. The new penology therefore aims to incarcerate for the longest time those groups of criminals that are most likely – defined statistically – to reoffend. It aspires to regulate and manage crime and criminals, but not to eliminate them or the causes of crime. The new penology simply manages a problem – a problem that is seen as, if not normal, then at least as a given which cannot be eradicated but instead must be managed, distributed and encapsulated as well as possible on the basis of actuarial knowledge. The same line of thought is visible in relation to surveillance and the management of the urban environment described above. Here also the underlying reasoning is that all humans are potentially criminal, and the aim is not to cure pathologies but simply to prevent. Therefore the key is to create environments which most hinder criminal behaviour. This often entails identifying high-risk zones by means of actuarial data and putting in place measures to reduce criminal behaviour in these zones.

O'Malley (2006) has argued that while actuarial techniques today play a much more predominant role in criminal justice, talk of a new actuarial penology might be exaggerated. Sentencing based solely on statistical assessments of the risk of reoffending is considered by many to lack the moral element of punishment. The judiciary has also objected to being reduced to little more than clerks looking up the right sentence in actuarial tables, and political initiatives such as 'three strikes and you're out' in fact work against the idea of an actuarial penology.

Many commentators (e.g. Garland, 2001; Hudson, 2003; O'Malley, 2006) nevertheless agree that actuarial concepts of risk have come to play a much more prominent role in the last twenty years or so, but not so much in regard to sentencing as in other areas of criminal justice. These areas include post-sentencing and correctional services, the latter of which is much more focused on the individual's so-called criminogenic needs – again based on actuarial assessments. In regard to post-sentencing, the US act known as 'Megan's Law' is the example most often mentioned. Megan's Law, named after a girl who was murdered by a person previously convicted of child molesting, stipulates that information about released sexual offenders – including photographs and addresses –

must be made available to the public; in that way members of the public will know whether they live close to anyone who was previously convicted of this type of crime. This information can be printed in newspapers and made public by other means – all states have the information available on the Internet. Frequent debates occur as to whether or not even tougher measures can be implemented; in spring 2007 the legislature in Ohio, for example, debated whether or not sexual offenders should be forced to have bright green licence plates on their cars.

Initiatives such as Megan's Law are based on ideas about risk and uncertainty in that the high statistical risk of sexual offenders reoffending has to a large extent legitimized these initiatives. Also, to a large extent the initiatives privatize or individualize risks insofar as they make information available to private citizens to enable them to protect themselves and their families. But there are other reasons for the initiatives. There has been, above all in American justice, a trend towards penal practices such as 'naming and shaming' or the reintroduction of the chain gang (Garland, 2001: 3). These practices are part of a 'tough on crime' discourse to which also belong such initiatives as the earlier mentioned 'three strikes and you're out'. Such practices share with actuarial penology and post-sentencing a break with therapeutic or rehabilitative forms of justice, but they are driven by a logic different from that of actuarial justice.

Examples such as Megan's Law raise urgent questions about traditional rights in liberal democracies. Being publicly exposed after having served one's sentence – after having paid one's dues to society – is a suspension of traditional liberal legal rights. Barbara Hudson has developed an elaborate critique of these new penal and crime prevention practices (Hudson, 2003). She emphasizes the connection between risks and individualization which is predominant in Becks's work and also in governmentality studies of liberalism, as we have already seen. She argues that the current conceptualization of risk in the legal system, coupled with individualization, undermines liberal ideals of justice and freedom. That is, conceptions of risk undermine classical liberal notions of freedom, and individualization undermines social liberal notions of solidarity.

Health and risk subjects

Some of the measures against terrorism and crime described above are practices that reduce liberty and are, in many cases, corporal. In many ways they roll back developments that have been seen as extensions of human and legal rights and the spread of ideas of correction and rehabilitation – in other words developments that have been seen as the continuing development of modernity. However, many of the initiatives cannot simply be seen as the rolling back of modernity and its ideals of liberty and rights. We saw in chapter 3 that one of the central achievements of the governmentality tradition is the development of an analysis of power of another sort, namely the type which involves the granting of freedom (Rose, 1999). These forms of disciplining consist of creating moral forms and subjectivities that conduct the conduct of free citizens. These forms of power and discipline are not corporal and do not rely on coercion, and they are above all government at a distance, but they shape conduct nevertheless. As Nikolas Rose writes,

> In advanced liberal societies, one family of control practices operates by affiliating subjects into a whole variety of practices in which the modulation of conduct according to certain norms is, as it were, designed in. These are the practices that Deleuze referred to in his thesis that we now live in 'societies of control' (1995). In disciplinary societies it was a matter of procession from one disciplinary institution to another – school, barracks, factory . . . – each seeking to mould conduct by inscribing enduring corporeal and behavioural competences, and persisting practices of self-scrutiny and self-constraint into the soul. Control society is one of constant and never-ending modulation where the modulation occurs within the flows and transactions between the forces and capacities of the human subject and the practices in which he or she participates. One is always in continuous training, life-long learning, perpetual assessment, continual incitement to buy, to improve oneself, constant monitoring of health and never-ending risk management. (Rose, 2000: 325)

Such government at a distance creates moral standards and forms of subjectivity in which the individual seeks the fulfilment of certain ambitions, desires and pleasures as well as the abolition of worries and problems. Modern subjectivities are influenced by a steady stream of expert advice on how to bring up children, be successful, grow as a person, have a good sex life, improve one's skills and, not least, stay healthy. The forces and capacities to which Rose refers and which shape subjects are increasingly expert discourses. Experts guide us to be better consumers, better parents, better learners, better citizens. But, also, we consume such advice – for example that found in newspapers or magazines (see chapter 7) – because we seek fulfilment of desires and reduction of worries. These forces are, of course, at the same time cultural. As in any culture, modern subjects are shaped by the meaning and values of their culture and condemned or sanctioned (however subtly) if they transgress. Mary Douglas's work is in fact a useful reminder that it is not only in today's society that power is exercised by, as Rose writes in the quotation above, 'affiliating subjects into a whole variety of practices in which the modulation of conduct according to certain norms is, as it were, designed in'. However, there is something distinctly new in the scope of the apparatus of expertise and knowledge which is amassed to gain knowledge about the population and provide citizens with information and knowledge. Moreover, culture is itself being targeted and intervened in precisely because of the recognition that culture shapes subjectivities, which means that culture must be changed in order to change conduct (Geary, 2007).

In relation to health, but not only in relation to health, risk features prominently. We are all, we saw in chapter 7, through the mass media and other information outlets, exposed to endless streams of information about health – advice and information about which practices pose health risks and which benefit our health. In the newspaper on the day of writing this there is a story about the risk of colon cancer due to excessive consumption of red meat. Such information moulds the behaviour of most of us; we are indeed encouraged actively to seek out the information, and we consume a variety of products and services in order to improve our health along the lines stipulated. Hence we take active responsibility for ourselves; we manage ourselves in the best possible way, avoiding risk factors.

The discourse on risks and health has many sources. In part, the information about health risks is the product of medical research and health professionals informing the public, often as parts of government campaigns. We saw in the previous chapter that the private insurance industry also plays a role, often in conjunction with public or private medical institutions, just as insurance companies may work together with law enforcement in relation to crime. But health is also a commercial industry, with journalists, physicians, lifestyle and nutrition consultants, and a range of other professionals providing information and services to consumers. This shows once again why we are dealing with government at a distance. Information flows about health and risk do not spring from one or a few central state agencies but are multibrooded. The information is often commodified, even to an extent that one may reasonably speculate whether the figure of the consumer perhaps plays a much more central role than that which it is granted in most of the literature on governmentality and health.

But of course we are not only dealing with markets where consumers buy information and expert advice in order to satisfy their desire for a healthy lifestyle and hence a long life with minimal risk. Another key issue when it comes to risks and health is the screening and risk prognostication techniques which are increasingly important in medical practices. New genetic screening techniques, for example, make it possible to identify genetic markers for a variety of diseases, including cancers and neurological diseases. Medicine has in other words created a whole new form of patient: 'persons genetically at risk' (Novas and Rose, 2000: 487). Such new screening techniques, Novas and Rose argue, create new and active relations between the individual and the future. This applies to a broad range of medical practices, and the implications are wide-ranging. It creates a whole new type of patient and subsequently a whole new terrain of medial intervention, where medicine is no longer concerned with curing the sick but with preventing the healthy from getting sick. We are no longer all potential patients. Instead we are all patients, whose potential illnesses must be prevented. This above all applies to those defined as being 'at risk'. Being defined as such means, of course, having to carry a heavy psychological burden (Hallowell, 2006); for some it is like living with a death sentence while at present being perfectly healthy. Needless to say, this scientific categorization exerts power. Like many other forms of medical discourse and practice, these new techniques force patients to engage actively with their future, to plan and to decide – for example to decide whether preventive surgery is needed. In most such cases there are no clear-cut guidelines as to when to opt for such measures, so patients are typically drawn into the decision-making process, if not left to decide for themselves. Certainly, this is a form of granting liberty to the individual patient, empowering her or him, but it also creates the imperative for the patient to become a responsible (risk) manager in relation to her or his own health. In chapter 5, when discussing public understanding of science, I referred to Barry, who remarked that citizens today were expected to be knowledgeable about scientific issues (Barry, 2001: 4). The same very much applies to medical matters. We are expected to be responsible, and are being made responsible, for our own health.

These last remarks have centred on medical practices and technologies, changes in the field of medical intervention expanding from the somatic into the presomatic, and the burdens this puts on people. But while they can be burdensome, the new medical services are certainly also being actively pursued. Genetic screenings are being purchased by people who wish to obtain knowledge about potential health dangers so that they can plan and actively work to avoid them (Lemke, 2004). Indeed, many of the themes discussed in the previous chapter emerge here as well: screening technologies and various other new technologies create a vast range of information relating to possible future events. Simultaneously, and at least in part subsequently, individuals (and institutions) are faced with an array of decisions, often involving consumption. Genetic screenings, insurance policies, stem cell samples and many of the other things mentioned here and in chapter 8 have in common that they involve future dangers which are rendered if not actual then at least sufficiently apprehendable that they can be acted on and insured against. And closely related to this is the development of a cultural narrative that celebrates individual control and individual action, be it climbing, taking out insurance, living healthily, gambling, skydiving, being an entrepreneur, undergoing screenings and so on. All of it has to do with figuring out individually the odds of the hand that has been dealt and optimizing its possibilities. Life has become a strategic enterprise (Novas and Rose, 2000: 487). Or, as Thomas Lempke puts it in the context of genetic screening, 'Rather than being viewed in terms of objective fate, genes today are increasingly seen to represent subjective potential: they refer to the supremacy of the consumer, who aims at profitable optimization of individual human capital and personal quality of life' (Lemke, 2004: 551).

Summary

New environmental and health risks have radically changed politics. Politics have, of course, always consisted of struggles over what the future should be like, with different ideologies presenting different, more or less utopian, versions. Risks politics arguably mark a change in this regard, as the struggles here are not so much over which future is best but over which future dangers must most urgently be avoided. And further to that, worries over risks have enhanced the scope of the political, expanding it beyond both traditional political institutions and national boundaries.

The political struggles are not just over definitions of the worst and best futures. Notions, and fears, of risks are also invoked to further political interests, and definitions and conceptualizations of risk change accordingly. Throughout this book, I have highlighted the ambiguity of risk, the morphing meanings of risk. These processes are intrinsically political. What I have also repeated often is that this ambiguity of risk does not make risk less important, or reduce it to simple questions about whether there is more risk or less, or to postulates that such risk politics is only based on the irrational fears of the public. There is a body of literature that focuses on what is called the 'culture of fear', and on the political use of such fear as a way of mobilizing support and furthering political interests (e.g. Altheide, 2002; 2006; Furedi, 2006). Such accounts build on the social amplification of risks framework (see chapter 6), but take a critical approach, arguing that the fears of risk are exaggerated; for example, these fears are inflated by economic or political elites who seek to further their own interests. Such explanations are little more than sociological versions of the psychometric notion of the dread factor, substituting psychological causes of amplified risk with social ones.

What this theoretical approach overlooks is not only the incontestable fact that technology today does impact the environment and human health in ways that are fraught with uncertainty. It also overlooks the fact that everyone fears something. Even though a given risk might cause panic in one country and indifference in another, the next time it could well prove the other way around. The difference is not between less or more fear but between fear of different things. Moreover, people do not fear things just because people are being manipulated by the ruling classes or whatever theoretical bogeyman is being constructed. Rather, people fear things that potentially endanger desired outcomes, and which outcomes are desirable hinges on values, not facts. Finally, there is no basis for claiming that fear of the future is more prevalent today than previously. The future, including future dangers, is certainly more *anticipated* today, but, as is also shown in chapter 8, this anticipation of the future also includes various strategies to exploit opportunities.

Such strategic relations to the future have surfaced in this chapter as well – here not in regard to edgework or economic entrepreneurship but in equally individualistic and strategic cultural imperatives to manage one's health. Increasingly, 'risks subjectivities' are being constructed that lead people to conduct themselves with a view to future possibilities. This 'responsibilization' is in many cases arguably a way of governing complexity. There are so many possibilities, so many potential dangers, that uniform guidelines and central decision making are impossible. Hence many decisions have to be taken individually, which in turn means that individuals must be made responsible and must plan their futures. I have in this chapter argued furthermore that the responsibilization in regard to such things as health is closely linked to the cultural narrative of control described in chapter 8. In both cases, individual control is valorized, and this valorization is key to a form of government where complexity means that much must be left under the control of the individual.

Importantly, developments such as those that have taken place in regard to health have radically reconfigured the relation between the public sector and private citizens. The vast knowledge about various risks – ironically often conveyed to the private citizen by public agencies – creates a new demand for risk reducing or risk-screening technologies which the public sector cannot satisfy. As we have also seen in relation to insurance generally, the culturally valorized strategic risk-reducing patient is turned into a consumer. Risk and uncertainty have been pivotal drivers of a political change reducing the importance of state welfare provision.

How these political and governmental changes have been driven by conceptions of risk and uncertainty has been best described by scholars working within the governmentality tradition. At the same time risk is also used in very different forms of government, in some cases not granting but rather stripping people of responsibility and freedom. The use of risk in government has, in regard to crime and terrorism, led to measures that represent a de-governmentalization, that is, government that is no longer from a distance and that no longer conducts conduct through the creation of subjectivities. Here we see incarcerations with no legal protection, the abolition of rights, torture, and public naming and shaming of criminals rather similar to what would happen in a medieval town square. Much of that happens in the name of risk management.

Risks can be used as political vehicles in many different ways, and talk of a culture of fear does not do this complexity justice. Wynne notes that risk is a specific discourse that allows members of the public to voice more general, but also more ambiguous, concerns over how society is developing (Wynne, 1996: 58). Wynne does not give examples, but one such might be GM technology; this technology draws protests not only because of the fear of risks but also because it can potentially alter nature in a way that clashes with many people's values about what nature is and how humans should engage with nature. Here, risk is a vehicle for voicing greater moral concerns. This adds ambiguity to the concept of risk, Wynne says, but this dimension needs to be recognized and is integral to a sociological understanding of what constitutes risk.

This chapter has shown a cosmopolitan impetus brought on by foreboding danger. Yet this development, which includes more international openness and the expansion of human rights, is countered by the highly problematic (seen from the point of view not only of cosmopolitanism but also of liberalism) tendencies that security measures bring. Above all, measures against the risk of terrorism and crime involve abolishing human rights, violating the sacredness of human life, and also stripping people of individual responsibilities and viewing them as little more than risk factors.

Barbara Hudson quotes Rorty in her thought-provoking critique of how such security measures undermine liberal principles, arguing like Rorty that solidarity and respect for the other hinge less on abstract notions of humanity and more on the little, mundane things that people recognize and realize that they share with strangers: loving their children, grieving over the death of loved ones and so on (Hudson, 2003: 223). It is worth noting that this is entirely consistent with a cosmopolitanism which highlights the everyday sense of coexistence rather than grand universals. It is also worth noting that Rorty has famously argued that solidarity is a product of proximity, of being within social and communicative proximity of others (Rorty, 1989). Public communication about risk, the global nature of these risks and especially media reports on risks and disasters might create both proximity and a feeling of sharing pain, grief and fear (Silverstone, 2007). But it is also possible that fear of risks may bring the opposite – mistrust, division and conflict.

In this regard it is worth returning to security. The risk of terrorism is not the only focal point for various governments attempting to provide security. Environmental risks, too, are increasingly securitized, that is, treated politically as threats to the stability of nations (Buzan, Wæver and Wilde, 1998: 71–93). This is the case in the United States, for example, where a law to combat global warming discussed in Congress in November 2007 is called America's Climate Security Act (ACSA). To a large extent, such a framing of global warming implies a focus on national security; and on the face of it, at least, this focus represents a stark contrast to Beck's hope for a more cosmopolitan world order, even though security measures can also include transnational cooperation and the creation of transnational institutions. I have throughout this book shown how the conception of risk is ambiguous. That case can be no greater than when it comes to how states act on some of the new global risks. Whether the end result will be more openness, liberalism and transnational cooperation or the very opposites remains to be seen. Beck's preoccupation with cosmopolitanism is not due to the fact that cosmopolitanism is empirically in evidence but because risks seem to create a development which could ultimately break in one of these two ways.

10
Conclusion

Categories of risk?

If one had to summarize this book in a single sentence, one could perhaps say that risk is both an enormous problem and a powerful concept. Risk ranks as a problem because new threats exist that not only have great magnitude and grave implications but also stymie political institutions ill-equipped to handle them. And it is perhaps not only the political institutions that are ill-equipped. It may be the case, too, that the general cognitive abilities of human beings to apprehend risks and to act against them are falling short, both individually and collectively and on both a scientific and a lay level. Scientists cannot replicate the time frames and the complexity of the causal processes set in motion by technology in laboratories and by computer simulations. The real tests are carried out not in the laboratories but in the ecosystem, and no one can know the outcomes because new technologies are introduced faster than the possible effects of the old can be scientifically established. In reality, our world has become one big laboratory. Moreover, for laypeople the scale of things is hard to fathom. It is hard to connect the threat of, say, global warming with the mundane task of driving the car to the supermarket for the weekend shopping, where groceries flown in from all over the world are on offer. Everywhere – in science and in laypeople's lives – the 'worm of culture' creeps in, filtering knowledge and facts through values and everyday routines.

As for its second incarnation, risk is literally a powerful concept. It renders areas of society governable; indeed, it has been central in creating the social as a space for government intervention. It is used to create common fears and enemies, to mobilize people, but it is also used for conducting conduct – for governing free subjects at a distance. Risk has legitimized drastic restrictions on human liberty, and, together with uncertainty, it has figured prominently in potent neoliberal political mentalities. These different forms of power and political thought are in some cases, but by no means always, connected. I have also shown how these last aspects evolve into a general cultural narrative – remembering, of course, with Douglas, that these always have to do with politics and power – which renders life (biological and biographical) a 'strategic enterprise' (Novas and Rose, 2000: 487).

Risks as concepts and as problems are not necessarily connected. Indeed, throughout the book a range of differences in the conceptualization of risks and the analysis of the consequences of risks has emerged. Among these were the differences between cosmopolitan openness and national closure, between liberal rights and security, between danger and opportunity, between risks as 'bads' and as 'goods', between therapeutic rehabilitation and risk profiling, and many others. One might argue that these differences hinge on distinctions between types of risk – for example, calculable risk and incalculable uncertainty – or that they hinge on the very distinction between risks as problems and as concepts. In fact, all the suggested differences translate into theoretical dittos, so maybe it is also a question of theoretical point of view? The theory of reflexive modernization focuses mainly on incalculable uncertainty and governmentality approaches, mainly on calculable risk.

To try to explain through such differences the multitude of guises that risk can assume is, however, unsustainable. To be sure, environmental uncertainties may trigger social and political dynamics different from those triggered by actuarial knowledge about crime risks, and crime and environmental risks are different phenomena, but in many cases these differences conflate. Environmental risks can become security issues, which means that the social and political dynamics they trigger will be rather similar to those triggered by crime, which is another security issue. Securitization in turn might mean national measures against other nations. But then again, not always. In any case, there are no set schemas for differentiating between types of risks and their consequences.

Much has been written here about the distinction between risks and uncertainty. To be sure, the distinction is important and analytically fruitful, but it is constantly conflated, not so much analytically but because potential dangers can involve both risk and uncertainty and because risk and uncertainty can have similar consequences. For example, when I have discussed how new penal technologies or anti-terror policies breach human rights, it is clear that this discussion involves both actuarial knowledge about crime and measures against more uncertain terror threats. We also saw in chapter 2 that understandings of risk can be conceptual rather than mathematical – but does that render it uncertainty rather than risk? Insurance in any case involves both, as described in chapter 8. Indeed, the entrepreneurial and adventurous culture – and by implication the risk society – described there cannot be described by either risk or uncertainty alone but by both, and, above all, by an orientation towards an open future that is a common denominator of risk and uncertainty.

Risks as potentials

One thing shared by the different theories is the realization that risk has markedly increased its presence – as problem and as concept – since the late 1960s, permeating almost all sectors of modern society. I have just discussed the diversity of the ways in which this has happened. One of the few connection points within this diverse range is that the awareness of, and ability to envisage, risk or uncertainty in all its forms corresponds to the awareness of, and ability to envisage, the future and its possibilities. This points to an intimate connection between risks and capitalism, it was suggested in chapter 8, because capitalism essentially is about investments in the future. Contemporary capitalism is arguably more 'future-oriented' than ever before, especially because more technologies now exist for calculating future possibilities which allow for more risk taking.

People have very different means of dealing with risks and their actual manifestations. They have very different means of anticipating how to deal with and exploit the future. The risk society is a future-oriented society where having the skills and the means to invest in the future, to approach and apprehend the future strategically, with discipline, foresight and care, is richly rewarded.

In his classic study of money, Georg Simmel describes money as being pure means, pure potential, that contains endless future possibilities (Simmel, 1990: 209–13). Apart from the fact that one should probably talk of capital rather than money, the implication is that economic means are potential goods while risks are potential dangers or 'bads'. This in turn means that capital (potential goods) can be used also to shield against (to outweigh) potential dangers. As we saw in chapter 6, socio-economically deprived people have little to hope for, little education, little human capital to invest in the future (in order to make it their future). For example, instead of embracing the chronology of education, then career, then relationship, then family – more or less, it seems, the planned life cycle of all middle-class Westerners – they instead seek instant pleasure and, in one sense at least, 'live for the moment'. Equally, insurance is a means for creating security, for keeping financially afloat and for staying in good health. Having secure housing is a means. For example, with more affluent people in the United States spending their retirement on the Atlantic coast, more people employed in the low-wage service sector are drawn to the area as well. These people often cannot afford houses and instead resort to mobile homes and other constructions that are much more vulnerable to hurricanes. They also cannot afford insurance, which adds to their vulnerability (Cutter and Emrich, 2006).

These are very real differences in possession of means. Such differences have arguably been ignored, perhaps not so much in risk research per se, but they do not feature heavily in major theories of risks. All of the 'big three' theories struggle with this topic. Beck's risk society thesis is arguably the one best equipped to include this aspect but nevertheless struggles, one reason being the idea that insurance is worth less in a risk society because new risks undermine the logic of compensation. But it is the opposite that seems to obtain: in a world full of risks, insurance is worth more, but it is therefore also more costly and therefore denied to more people. Beck nevertheless does have a very sharp eye for how social inequality amounts also to inequality of risk exposure.

Cultural theory of risk trains a sharp eye on differences, but these are cultural differences leading to differences in opinion and preferences. How these connect with material differences is much less clear; indeed, it seems outside the scope of the theory. Moreover, the individual's ability to act strategically, to invest in the future, receives little attention in this theoretical approach. The governmentality approach is also ill-suited to thinking through these aspects. It is less interested in real potential dangers than in their conceptualizations, and it is more interested in how risks create spaces for government (for anything to be a governable unit it has to have some form of unity or homogeneity) than it is interested in differences.

Risk, responsibility and individualization

Apart from both relating to possible futures, do health and environmental risks overlap at all with entrepreneurial risk taking? Yes, they do, and in two ways. First, some of the risks ventured by entrepreneurial risk discourse are of course possible side effects of technology and science. Both industry and governments in most European countries have expressed concerns over public resistance to new technologies, arguing that economic strength depends on technological development, which means that risk aversion will hamper not only technological but also economic development. What is called for, in other words, is some public acceptance of entrepreneurial risk taking, and not only the taking of economic risks. Political discussions are subsequently over how great these risks should be.

Second, the risk and uncertainties of technology and of medical practices, and the entrepreneurial embrace of uncertainty most often have the same effect – namely that individuals have to assume more responsibility for themselves. In chapter 1, I wrote how the difference between risks and random dangers hinges on human action, decisions and knowledge. Even though the uncertainties described in this book are also random, or at least escape probabilistic knowledge, they are not the same as random dangers. The reason is that such uncertainties involve action, decisions and knowledge. In that regard, risk and uncertainty merge. Whether or not the potential dangers are calculable, they are, so to speak, 'on the radar', they are subject to human action – indeed, they demand human action.

This puts pressure on governments, on organizations and on individuals – in fact, not least on individuals. In fact, individualization of risk seems to mean privatization – as opposed to the public (state) forms of insurance which emerged in the industrial epoch when risk became a public (state) concern. The complexities of risks and uncertainties mean that government has given up the idea of being, to paraphrase Bauman (1987), a gardener in the garden called society, carefully controlling all growth by seeding, planting, weeding and nurturing. Instead, more is left to the individual and to the markets. As a result, whether in science, politics, medicine or the market, each person is increasingly being asked – I deliberately put this in market and gambling lingo – to take his or her own position, and to manage his or her own future in the best way possible. Universal guidelines are increasingly hard to come by; the imperative is 'make your own' (and thereby take your own chances). In this regard, the governmentality approach and Beck's theory of reflexive modernization concur. Institutional individualism is a governmental imperative; manage your life, with all its risk and uncertainties, individually.

Where to, risk?

Asking what will happen with risk in the future brings, of course, the immediate answer that risks which are potential dangers now will materialize later – as dangers, disasters or problems. This logical answer might be something sociology will have to bear in mind. The nature of risks as potentials does not make them unreal, I have argued, but they are certainly latent. The sociology of risk has successfully studied the uncertainties surrounding such latent risks, and with equally great success analysed risk as a concept or element in thought that translates into technologies of government. But some risks do materialize, for example, as holes in the ozone layer around the poles or as global warming. In a sense, the concept of risks pushes such disasters ahead of us, keeping them in the future. The meaning conveyed by risk is that the disasters have not happened yet. But perhaps we increasingly must ask ourselves if some of these disasters have not already occurred, if we are not living in, if not a post-apocalyptic age, then in an age of disaster in which the sense of normality has been seriously skewed. Weather reports today often feature updates on the thick(or thin)ness of the ozone layer and issue warnings against sun exposure on days when there are particularly high levels of UV radiation. Today, this is normal. Or is this normal?

Of course new potential but uncertain dangers will crop up, but above all the risk of global warming seems at the moment to be changing from being a risk to a known danger of immense scale. The social consequences might be equally staggering. Risks no doubt create a sense of collectivity, a community of risks. We look for collective solutions to them, and unite against those who potentially threaten us. Yet when risks materialize, they perhaps tend to become less collective – they are disasters and misfortunes befalling individuals and nations. We collectively face the risks of cancer due to the pollution of our environment, but we suffer from cancer individually. We all face the risks of global warming, but some nations and regions (and individuals) will suffer more than others. The question is what unites us more: sharing the risk or feeling compassion for those actually devastated by the disasters? And the question is, above all, what happens to solidarity once risks become manifest? As for global warming, interesting but also absurd things can already be observed. With the polar ice caps melting, countries are gearing up for political struggles over ownership of the Arctic and Antarctic, laying claim to small, hitherto insignificant, islands or disputing the geography of the seabed. The reason is that as the ice melts the pole's natural resources become accessible. Chief among these resources is of course oil, a fossil fuel which when used will increase carbon dioxide emissions still further.

In spite of such examples of national interests flourishing in the face of collective dangers, it is an indisputable fact that risks create transnational political cooperation. The transnational regimes described in chapter 9 testify to that. It is far more difficult to pinpoint the cultural changes, the changes in people's outlook, the sense of a shared fate in the face of global threats. Yet there is little doubt that fundamental changes have occurred, that mass media reports on risks bring people from around the world closer together, that global risks do create a new cosmopolitan feeling.

But, as chapter 9 in particular showed, policies built around notions of risk also point in the other direction – to measures that reduce mobility (Packer, 2006; Shamir, 2005), create new boundaries and restrict civil rights that looked as though they might soon become universal. More than anything a new awareness of the risk of terror has led governments around the world to take initiatives to reduce and monitor movements and to screen visitors. This contradiction is somewhat perplexing – can risk really cause both cosmopolitanism and fear of strangers? The answer probably is yes; risk can take many different meanings and can lead to different attitudes, different policies and strategies. The argument throughout this book has been that risks are not pure ontological entities, not simple real problems but also in part socially constructed. Or perhaps – in an attempt to go beyond the quite frankly tedious concept of social constructionism – one could say that risks are associations, couplings of material problems and human understandings. Such associations evolve in an unruly fashion, and so do the frames with which humans make sense of them. With risks being constantly mutating associations, they necessarily extend into an unknown future. Indeed risk (and uncertainty) is precisely a concept which humans associate with an uncertain future. They can do so in many different ways: the framing and conceptualizations of risks can vary, and themselves mutate, and they can be a part, even a cornerstone, of very different political, social and economic configurations. Therefore risks can be entrepreneurial opportunities or threats to civilization. And therefore the same specific risk, say global warming, can lead to a new cosmopolitan order or to national security measures. It should really come as no surprise that risks, which more than anything else epitomize uncertainty and unpredictability, themselves have unpredictable trajectories. What, however, does seem relatively certain – and to show this has been the great achievement of sociologies of risks – is that risk will continue to permeate social life in the future as well. Given this decisive but uncertain role, it seems not overly grandiose to conclude that the future of modernity to a large extent depends on the ways in which risks are understood and which solutions to them are found.

References

Adam, B. (1998). *Timescapes of Modernity*. London: Routledge.

Agamben, G. (1998). *Homo Sacer*. Stanford: Stanford University Press.

Alexander, J. C. and J. L. Mast (2006). Introduction: symbolic action in theory and practice: the cultural pragmatics of symbolic action, in J. C. Alexander, B. Giesen and J. L. Mast (eds.), *Social Performance, Symbolic Action, Cultural Pragmatics, and Ritual*. Cambridge: Cambridge University Press, 1–28.

Altheide, D. (2002). *Creating Fear*. New York: Aldine de Gruyter.

Altheide, D. (2006). Terrorism and the Politics of Fear. *Cultural Studies*, 6 (4), 415–39.

Andersen, A. and R. Ott (1988). Risikoperception im industriali-seringszeitalter am Beispiel des Hüttenwesens. *Archiv für Sozialgeschichte*, 28, 75–109.

Anderson, A. (2006). Media and risk, in G. Mythen and S. Walklate (eds.), *Beyond the Risk Society*. Maidenhead: Open University Press, 114–31.

Arnoldi, J. (2003). Making Sense of Causation. *Soziale Welt*, 54 (4), 405–27.

Arnoldi, J. (2004). Derivatives – Virtual Values and Real Risks. *Theory, Culture and Society*, 21 (6), 23–42.

Arnoldi, J. (2007). Universities and the Public Recognition of Expertise. *Minerva*, 45, 49–61.

Baker, T. and Simon, J. (2002). *Embracing Risk*. Chicago: University of Chicago Press.

Baker, T. (2003). Containing the Promise of Insurance: Adverse Selection and Risk Classification, in R. V. Ericson and A. Doyle (eds.), *Risk and Morality*. Toronto: University of Toronto Press, 258–83.

Baker, T. (2004). Risk, Insurance, and the Social construction of Responsibility, in T. Baker and J. Simon (eds.), *Embracing Risk*. Chicago: University of Chicago Press, 33–51.

Barke, R. P., H. Jenkins-Smith and P. Slovic (1997). Risk Perceptions of Men and Women Scientists. *Social Science Quarterly*, 78 (1), 167–77.

Barry, A. (2001). *Political Machines*. London: Athlone.

Bauman, Z. (1987). *Legislators and Interpreters*. Cambridge: Polity Press.

Bauman, Z. (2000). *Liquid Modernity*. Cambridge: Polity Press.

Beck, U. (1986). *Risikogesellschaft*. Frankfurt am Main: Suhrkamp.

Beck, U. (1992). *Risk Society – Towards a New Modernity*. London: Sage.

Beck, U. (1997). *The Reinvention of Politics*. Cambridge: Polity Press.

Beck, U. (1998). Politics of Risk Society, in J. Franklin (ed.), *The Politics of Risk Society*. Cambridge: Polity Press, 9–22.

Beck, U. (1999). *What is Globalization?*. Cambridge: Polity Press.

Beck, U. (2000). Risk Society Revisited: Theory, Politics, and Research Programmes, in B. Adam, U. Beck and J. V. Loon (eds.), *The Risk Society and Beyond*. London: Sage, 211–29.

Beck, U. (2004). *Der Kosmopolitische Blick oder: Krieg ist Frieden*. Frankfurt am Main: Suhrkamp.

Beck, U. (2007). *Weltrisikogesellschaft*. Frankfurt am Main: Suhrkamp.

Beck, U. and E. Grande (2004). *Das Kosmopolitische Europa*. Frankfurt am Main: Suhrkamp.

Beck, U. and N. Znaider (2006). Unpacking Cosmopolitanism for the Social Sciences: A Research Agenda. *British Journal of Sociology*, 57 (1), 1–23.

Beck, U., A. Giddens and S. Lash (1994). *Reflexive Modernization*. Cambridge: Polity Press.

Bernstein, P. L. (1992). *Capital Ideas*. New York: Free Press.

Bernstein, P. L. (1996). *Against the Gods*. New York: John Wiley.

Björnstén, U. (2006). Science Writing in the Risk Society: The Mobile Phone Case, paper presented at the conference *Science and Democracy*, Stockholm, March 2006,.

Boholm, Å. (2003). The Cultural Nature of Risk: Can There Be an Anthropology of Uncertainty? *Ethnos*, 68 (2), 159–78.

Bollig, M. (2006). *Risk Management in a Hazardous Environment: A Comparative Study of Two Pastoral Societies*. New York: Springer Verlag.

Bonfadelli, H. (2005). Mass Media and Biotechnology: Knowledge Gaps within and between European Countries. *International Journal of Public Opinion Research*, 17 (1), 42–62.

Bonß, W. (1995). *Vom Risiko*. Hamburg: Hamburger Edition.

Bougen, P. D. (2003). Catastrophe Risk. *Economy and Society*, 32 (2), 253–74.

Briggs, C. M. (2006). Science and Environmental Risks: The Case of Perchlorate Contamination in California. *Environmental Politics*, 15 (4), 532–49.

Bröckling, U. (2005). Gendering the Enterprising Self. *Distinktion*, 11, 11–25.

Brown, N. and M. Michael (2002). From Authority to Authenticity: The Changing Governance of Biotechnology. *Health, Risk and Society*, 4 (3), 259–72.

Buzan, B., O. Wæver and J. d. Wilde (1998). *Security: A New Framework for Analysis*. Boulder: Lynne Rienner Publishers.

Callon, M. (1998). *The Laws of the Market*. Oxford: Blackwell.

Clark, B. and R. York (2005). Dialectical Materialism and Nature: An Alternative to Economism and Deep Ecology. *Organization and Environment*, 18 (3), 318–37.

Comaroff, J. and J. L. Comaroff (2000). Millennial Capitalism. *Public Culture*, 12 (2), 291–343.

Cook, T. (1998). *Governing with the News*. Chicago: University of Chicago Press.

Couldry, N. (2003). Media Meta-capital: Extending the Range of Bourdieu's Field Theory. *Theory and Society*, 32, 653–77.

Cutter, S. L. and C. T. Emrich (2006). Moral Hazard, Social Catastrophe: The Changing Face of Vulnerability along the Hurricane Coasts. *Annals of the American Academy*, 604, 102–12.

Daston, L. (1988). *Classical Probability in the Enlightenment*. Princeton: Princeton University Press.

Dean, M. (1999). *Governmentality*. London: Sage.

Dijk, T. A. van (1985). Structures of News in the Press, in T. A. v. Dijk (ed.) *Discourse and Communication*. Berlin: de Gruyter, 69–93).

Dijk, T. A. van (1988a). *News as Discourse*. Hillsdale: New Jersey.

Dijk, T. A. van (1988b). *News Analysis*. Hillsdale: Lawrence Erlbaum Associates.

Douglas, M. (1982). Introduction to Grid Group Analysis, in M. Douglas (ed.), *Essays in the Sociology of Perception*. London: Routledge & Kegan Paul, 1–8.

Douglas, M. (1984). *Purity and Danger*. London: Routledge & Kegan Paul.

Douglas, M. (1986). *Risk Acceptabillity According to the Social Sciences*. London: Routledge & Kegan Paul.

Douglas, M. (1987). *How Institutions Think*. London: Routledge & Kegan Paul.

Douglas, M. (1992). *Risk And Blame*. London: Routledge.

Douglas, M. and A. Wildawsky (1983). *Risk and Culture*. Berkeley: University of California Press.

Drori, G. S., J. W. Meyer, F. O. Ramirez and E. Schofer (2003). *Science in the Modern World Polity*. Stanford: Stanford University Press.

Dunlap, R. (1997). The Evolution of Environmental Sociology: A Brief Assessment of the American Experience, in M. Redclift and G. Woodgate (eds.), *The International Handbook of Environmental Sociology*. Cheltenham: Edward Elgar, 21–39.

Dunlap, R. E. (1998). Lay Perceptions of Global Risks. *International Sociology*, 13 (4), 473–98.

Eden, S. (1998). Environmental Issues: Knowledge, Uncertainty and the Environment. *Progress in human geography*, 22 (3), 425–32.

Eldridge, J., J. Kitzinger and K. William (1997). *The Mass Media and Power in Modern Britain*. Oxford: Oxford University Press.

Ericson, R. V. and A. Doyle (2003). *Risk and Morality*. Toronto: University of Toronto Press.

Ericson, R. V. and A. Doyle (2004a). Catastrophe Risk, Insurance and Terrorism. *Economy and Society*, 33 (2), 135–73.

Ericson, R. V. and A. Doyle (2004b). *Uncertain Business*. Toronto: University of Toronto Press.

Ericson, R. V., A. Doyle and D. Barry (2003). *Insurance as Governance*. Toronto: Toronto University Press.

Eve, R. A., S. Hornsfall and M. E. Lee (1997). *Chaos, Complexity and Sociology*. Thousand Oaks: Sage.

Ewald, F. (1991). Insurance and Risk, in G. Burchell, C. Gordon and P. Miller (eds.), *The Foucault Effect*. Hemel Hempstead: Harvester Wheatsheaf, 197–210.

Ewald, F. (1993a). *Der Vorsorgestaat*. Frankfurt am Main: Suhrkamp.

Ewald, F. (1993b). Two Infinities of Risk, in B. Massumi (ed.), *The Politics of Everyday Fear*. Minneapolis: University of Minnesota Press.

Ewald, F. (2002). The Return of Descartes's Malicious Demon: An Outline of a Philosophy of Precaution, in T. Baker and J. Simon (eds.), *Embracing Risk*. Chicago: University of Chicago Press, 273–301.

Featherstone, M. (1991). *Consumer Culture and Postmodernism*. London: Sage.

Feeley, M. M. and J. Simon (1992). The New Penology: Notes on the Emerging Strategy of Corrections and its Implications. *Criminology*, 30 (4), 449–74.

Felt, U. (2000). Why Should the Public 'Understand' Science?, in M. Dierkes and C. v. Grote (eds.), *Between Understanding and Trust*. Amsterdam: Harwood Academic Publishers, 7–38.

Fisher, D. R. (2003). Global and Domestic Actors within the Global Climate Change Regime. *International Journal of Sociology and Social Policy*, 23 (10), 5–30.

Flynn, J., P. Slovic and H. Kunreuther (2001). *Risk, Media and Stigma*. London: Earthscan.

Foucault, M. (1970). *The Order of Things*. New York: Vintage Books.

Foucault, M. (1983). The Subject and Power, in H. L. Dreyfus and P. Rabinow (eds.), *Michel Foucault – Beyond Structuralism and Hermeneutics*. Chicago: The University of Chicago Press.

Foucault, M. (1991). Governmentality, in G. Burchell, C. Gordon and P. Miller (eds.), *The Foucault Effect*. London: Harvester Wheatsheaf.

Franklin, J. (2001). *The Science of Conjecture*. Baltimore: Johns Hopkins University Press.

Funtowitcz, S. O. and J. R. Ravetz (1993). Science of the Post-normal Age. *Futures*, 25 (7), 739–55.

Furedi, F. (2006). *Culture of Fear Revisited: Risk-Taking and the Morality of Low Expectation*. London: Continuum.

Furstenberg, G. v. (1990). *Acting under Uncertainty*. Norwell: Kluwer Academic Publishers.

Garland, D. (2001). *Culture of Control: Crime and Social Order in Contemporary Society*. Oxford: Oxford University Press.

Garland, D. (2003). The Rise of Risk, in R. V. Ericson and A. Doyle (eds.), *Risk and Morality*. Toronto: University of Toronto Press, 48–83.

Geary, A. (2007). Culture as an Object of Ethical Governance in AIDS Prevention. *Cultural Studies*, 21 (4–5), 672–94.

Geertz, C. (1973). *The Interpretation of Cultures*. New York: Basic Books.

Gergen, K. J. (1998). Constructionist Dialogues and the Vicissitudes of the Political, in I. Velody and R. Williams (eds.), *The Politics of Constructionism*. London: Sage, 33–48.

Giddens, A. (1990). *The Consequences of Modernity*. Cambridge: Polity Press.

Giddens, A. (1991). *Modernity and Self-Identity*. Cambridge: Polity Press.

Giddens, A. (1999). *Runaway World*. London: Profile Books.

Gigenrenzer, G., Z. Swijtink, T. Porter, L. Daston, J. Beatty and L. Krüger (1989). *The Empire of Chance*. Cambridge: Cambridge University Press.

Gilbert, G. N. and M. Mulkay (1984). *Opening Pandora's Box*. Cambridge: Cambridge University Press.

Gillespie, B., D. Eva and R. Johnston (1979). Carcinogenic Risk Assessment in the United States and Great Britain: The Case of Aldrin/Dieldrin. *Social Studies of Science*, 9, 265–301.

Goffman, E. (1974). *Frame Analysis*. New York: Harper & Row.

Grande, E. and L. W. Pauly (2005). *Complex Sovereignty*. Toronto: University of Toronto Press.

Green, E. E. (2002). Narratives of Risk: Women at Midlife, Medical 'Experts' and Health Tehnologies. *Health, Risk and Society*, 4 (3), 273–86.

Hacking, I. (1975). *The Emergence of Probability*. Cambridge: Cambridge University Press.

Hacking, I. (1990). *The Taming of Chance*. Cambridge: Cambridge University Press.

Hacking, I. (1999). *The Social Construction of What?* Cambridge: Harvard University Press.

Hacking, I. (2003). Risk and Dirt, in R. V. Ericson and A. Doyle (eds.), *Risk and Morality*. Toronto: University of Toronto Press, 22–47.

Hallowell, N. (2006). Varieties of Suffering: Living with the Risk of Ovarian Cancer. *Health, Risk and Society*, 8 (1), 9–26.

Hansen, A. (1993). Introduction, in A. Hansen (ed.), *The Mass Media and Environmental Issues*. Leicester: Leicester University Press, xv–xxii.

Hansson, S. O. (2002). Uncertainties in the Knowledge Society. *International Social Science Journal*, 54 (1), 39–46.

Hier, S. P. (2002). Raves, Risks and the Ecstacy Panic: A Case Study in the Subversive Nature of Moral Regulation. *Canadian Journal of Sociology*, 27 (1), 33–57.

Hironaka, A. (2003). Science and the Environment, in G. S. Drori, J. W. Meyer, F. O. Ramirez and E. Schofer (eds.), *Science in the Modern World Polity*. Stanford: Stanford University Press, 249–64.

Holzer, B. and M. P. Sørensen (2003). Rethinking Subpolitics: Beyond the 'Iron Cage' of Modern Politics? *Theory, Culture and Society*, 20 (2), 79–102.

Hood, C., H. Rothstein and R. Baldwin (2004). *Goverment of Risk*. Oxford: University of Oxford Press.

Hudson, B. (2003). *Justice in a Risk Society*. London: Sage.

Hughes, E., J. Kitzinger and G. Murdock (2004). The Media and Risk, in P. Taylor-Gooby and J. O. Zinn (eds.), *Risk in Social Science*. Oxford: Oxford University Press, 250–70.

Intergovernmental Panel on Climate Change (2007). Summary for Policy Makers. Brussels: VMO/UNEP.

Irwin, A. (1989). Deciding about Risk, in J. Brown (ed.), *Environmental Threats*. London: Belhaven Press, 19–32.

Irwin, A. (2001). Constructing the Scientific Citizen. *Public Understanding of Science* (10), 1–18.

Jasanoff, S. (1987). Contested Boundaries in Policy-Relevant Science. *Social Studies of Science*, 17 (2), 195–230.

Jasanoff, S. (1993). Bridging the Two Cultures of Risk Analysis. *Risk Analysis*, 13 (2), 123–9.

Jasanoff, S. (1997). American Exeptionalism and the Political Acknowledgement of Risk, in S. Jasanoff (ed.), *Comparative Science and Technology Policy*. Cheltenham: Edward Elgar Publishing, 391–411.

Jasanoff, S. (2002). Citizens at Risk: Cultures of Modernity in the US and the EU. *Science as Culture*, 11 (3), 363–80.

Jasanoff, S. (2006). Risk in Hindsight – Towards a Politics of Reflection, in I. K. Richter, S. Berking and R. Milller-Schmid (eds.), *Risk Society and the Culture of Precaution*. Basingstoke: Palgrave Macmillan, 28–46.

Kasperson, J. X., R. E. Kasperson, N. Pidgeon and P. Slovic (2003). The Social Amplification of Risk: Assessing 15 Years of Research, in N. Pidgeon, R. E. Kasperson and P. Slovic (eds.), *The Social Amplification of Risk*. Cambridge: Cambridge University Press, 13–46.

Kasperson, J. X. and R. E. Kasperson (2005). *The Social Contours of Risk*. London: Earthscan.

Kasperson, J. X., R. E. Kasperson, B. L. Turner, W. Hsieh and A. Schiller (2005). Vulnerability to Global Environmental Change, in J. X. Kasperson and R. E. Kasperson (eds.), *The Social Contours of Risk, Volume II: Risk Analysis, Corporations and the Globalization of Risk*. London: Earthscan, 243–85.

Kitzinger, J. (2004). *Framing Abuse*. London: Pluto Press.

Knight, Frank H. (2006). *Risk, Uncertainty and Profit*. Mineola: Dover Publications.

Knorr-Cetina, K. (2000). Postsocial Theory, in G. Ritzer and B. Smart (eds.), *Handbook of Social Theory*. London: Sage, 520–37.

Koné, D. and E. Mullet (1994). Societal Risk Perception and Media Coverage. *Risk Analysis*, 14 (1), 21–4.

Krüger, L. (1987). The Probabilistic Revolution in Physics – An Overview, in L. Krüger, L. J. Daston and M. Heidelberger (eds.), *The Probabilistic Revolution*. Cambridge: MIT Press, 373–8.

Lash, S. (2002). *Critique of Information*. London: Sage.

Latour, B. (1990). Postmodern? No, Simply Amodern! Steps towards an Anthropology of Science. *Studies in the History and Philosophy of Science*, 21 (1), 145–71.

Latour, B. (1993). *We Have Never Been Modern*. New York: Harvester Wheatsheaf.

Latour, B. (1998). To Modernize or to Ecologize? That's the Question, in N. Castree and B. Willems-Braun (eds.), *Remaking Reality: Nature at the Millenium*. London: Routledge, 221–42.

Latour, B. (1999). On Recalling ANT, in J. Law and J. Hassard (eds.), *Actor Network Theory and After*. Oxford: Blackwell, 15–25.

Latour, B. (2000). When Things Strike Back. *British Journal of Sociology*, 51 (1), 105–23.

Latour, B. (2003). Is *Re*-modernization Occurring – And If So, How to Prove It? *Theory, Culture and Society*, 20 (2), 35–48.

Latour, B. (2004). *Politics of Nature*. Cambridge, MA: Harvard University Press.

Law, J. (1999). After ANT: Complexity, Naming and Topology, in J. Law and J. Hassard (eds.), *Actor Network Theory and After*. Oxford: Blackwell, 1–14.

Law, J. and A. Mol (2002). *Complexities*. Durham, NC: Duke University Press.

Leach, M., I. Scoones and B. Wynne (2005). Introduction: Science, Citizenship and Globalization, in M. Leach, I. Scoones and B. Wynne (eds.), *Science and Citizens*. London: Zed Books, 3–14.

Lemke, T. (2004). Disposition and Determinism – Genetic Diagnostics in Risk Society. *Sociological Review*, 52 (4), 550–66.

Leslie, J. and G. Wyatt (1992). Futures and Options, in D. Cobham (ed.), *Markets and Dealers: The Economics of the London Financial Markets*. London: Arnold, 85–110.

Levidow, L. (2002). Precautionary Uncertainty: Regulating GM Crops in Europe. *Social Studies of Science*, 31 (6), 842–74.

Lind, U. and J. Arnoldi (2006). Tro, håb og stamceller, in L. Koch and K. Høyer (eds.), *Håbets Teknologi*. Copenhagen: Munksgaard, 157–78.

Linder, S. H. (2006). Cashing-in on Risk Claims: On the For-Profit Inversion of Signifiers for 'Global . Warming'. *Social Semiotics*, 16 (1), 103–32.

Lipuma, E. and B. Lee (2004). *Financial Derivatives and the Globalization of Risk*. Durham, NC: Duke University Press.

Loon, J. V. (2002). *Risk and Technological Culture*. London: Routledge.

Luhmann, N. (1993). *Risk – A Sociological Theory*. New York: De Gruyter.

Luhmann, N. (1995). *Social Systems*. Stanford: Stanford University Press.

Luhmann, N. (1997). *Die Gesellschaft der Gesellschaft*. Frankfurt am Main: Suhrkamp.

Luhmann, N. (1998). *Observations on Modernity*. Stanford: Stanford University Press.

Luhmann, N. (2000). *The Reality of the Mass Media*. Cambridge: Polity Press.

Lupton, D. (1999). *Risk*. Abingdon: Routledge.

Lupton, D. (2004). 'A Grim Health Future': Food Risks in the Sydney Press. *Health, Risk and Society*, 6 (2), 187–200.

Lupton, D. (2006). Sociology and Risk, in G. Mythen and S. Walklate (eds.), *Beyond the Risk Society*. Maidenhead: Open University Press, 11–24.

Lynch, M. (1998). The Discursive Production of Uncertainty. *Social Studies of Science*, 24 (5–6), 829–68.

Lyng, S. (1990). Edgework: A Social Psychological Analysis of Voluntary Risk Taking. *American Journal of Sociology*, 95 (4), 851–86.

Lyng, S. (2005). Edgework and the Risk-Taking Experience, in S. Lyng (ed.), *Edgework, the Sociology of Risk Taking*. New York: Routledge, 3–14.

McComas, K. and J. Shanahan (1999). Telling Stories about Climate Change. *Communication Research*, 26 (1), 30–57.

McGuigan, J. (2005). Culture and Risk, in G. Mythen and S. Walklate (eds.), *Beyond the Risk Society*. Maidenhead: Open University Press, 211–30.

MacKenzie, D. and Y. Millo (2003). Constructing a Market, Performing Theory: The Historical Sociology of a Financial Derivatives Exchange. *American Journal of Sociology*, 109 (1), 107–45.

McLaughlin, A. (1993). *Regarding Nature*. Albany: State University of New York Press.

Macnaghten, P. and J. Urry (1997). *Contested Natures*. London: Sage.

Malone, R. E., E. Boyd and L. A. Bero (2000). Science in the News. *Social Studies of Science*, 30 (5), 713–35.

Mason, M. (2005). *The New Accountability*. London: Earthscan.

Mazur, A. (1998). Global Environmental Change in the News. *International Sociology*, 13 (4), 457–72.

Meek, J. (2002). Everyone has a voice. *London Review of Books*, 24 (13), 8–10.

Merton, R. K. (1987). Three Fragments from a Sociologist's Notebooks: Establishing the Phenomenon., Specified Ignorance and Strategic Research Materials. *Annual Review of Sociology*, 13 (1), 1–28

Mol, A. P. (2003). *The Ecological Modernization of the Global Economy*. Cambridge, MA: MIT Press.

Murphy, J., L. Levidow and S. Carr (2006). Regulatory Standards for Environmental Risks. *Social Studies of Science*, 36 (1), 133–60.

Murphy, R. (1997). *Sociology and Nature*. Boulder: Westview Press.

Mythen, G. and S. Walklate (2005). Criminology and Terrorism. *British Journal of Criminology*, 46 (1), 379–98.

Nelkin, D. (1992). *Controversy*. Newbury Park: Sage.

Nerone, J. and K. G. Barnhurst (2003). News Form and the Media Environment: A Network of Represented Relationships. *Media, Culture, and Society*, 25 (1), 111–24.

Novas, C. and N. Rose (2000). Genetic Risk and the Birth of the Somatic Individual. *Economy and Society*, 29 (4), 485–513.

Nowotny, H. (1994). *Time – The Modern and Postmodern Experience*. Cambridge: Polity Press.

Nowotny, H. (2000). Transgressive Competence. *European Journal of Social Theory*, 3 (1), 5–21.

Nowotny, H., P. Scott and M. Gibbons (2001). *Re-thinking Science – Knowledge and the Public in an Age of Uncertainty*. Cambridge: Polity Press.

O'Malley, P. (1998a). Risk, Power and Crime Prevention, in P. O'Malley (ed.), *Crime and Risk Society*. Aldershot: Ashgate, 71–93.

O'Malley, P. (ed.) (1998b). *Crime and Risk Society*. Aldershot: Ashgate.

O'Malley, P. (2000). Uncertain Subjects: Risks, Liberalism and Contracts. *Economy and Society*, 29 (4), 460–84.

O'Malley, P. (2003). Moral Uncertainties, in R. V. Ericsson and A. Doyle (eds.), *Risk and Morality*. Toronto: University of Toronto Press, 231–57.

O'Malley, P. (2004). *Risk, Uncertainty, and Government*. London: Glasshouse Press.

O'Malley, P. (2006). Criminology and Risk, in G. Mythen and S. Walklate (eds.), *Beyond the Risk Society*. Maidenhead: Open University Press, 43–59.

Ortner, S. B. (1997). Thick Resistance: Death and the Cultural Construction of Agency in Himalayan Mountaineering. *Representations*, 59 (4), 135–62.

Osborne, T. (2004). On Mediators: Intellectuals and the Ideas Trade in the Knowledge Society. *Economy and Society*, 33 (4), 430–47.

Ottway, H. (1992). Public Wisdom, Expert Fallibility: Toward a Contextual Theory of Risk, in S. Krimsky and D. Golding (eds.), *Social Theories of Risk* , 215–28. Westport: Praeger.

Packer, J. (2006). Becoming Bombs: Mobilizing Mobility in the War on Terror. *Cultural Studies*, 20 (4–5), 378–99.

Parker, J. and H. Stanworth (2005). Go for It! Towards a Critical Realist Approach to Voluntary Risk-Taking. *Health, Risk and Society*, 7 (4), 319–36.

Parnaby, P. (2007). Crime Prevention through Environmental Design: Financial Hardship, the Dynamics of Power, and the Prospects of Governance. *Crime, Law and Social Change*, 48 (1), 73–85.

Paterson, M. (2001). Risky Business: Insurance Companies in Global Warming Politics. *Global Environmental Politics*, 1 (4), 18–42.

Perrow, C. (1984). *Normal Accidents*. New York: Basic Books.

Peters, H. P. (1995). The Interaction of Journalists and Scientific Experts: Co-operation and Conflict between Two Professional Cultures. *Media, Culture and Society*, 17, 31–48.

Prigogine, I. (1980). *From Being to Becoming*. New York: W. H Freeman.

Prigogine, I. (1997). *The End of Certainty – Time, Chaos, and the New Laws of Nature*. New York: Free Press.

Prigogine, I. and I. Stengers (1984). *Order Out of Chaos – Man's New Dialogue with Nature*. London: Heinemann.

Rayner, S. (1992). Cultural Theory and Risk Analysis, in S. Krimsky and D. Golding (eds.), *Social Theories of Risk*. Westport: Praeger, 83–115.

Reith, G. (1999). *The Age of Chance*. London: Routledge.

Reith, G. (2004). Uncertain Times – The Notion of 'Risk' and the Development of Modernity. *Time and Society*, 13 (2/3), 383–402.

Reith, G. (2005). On the Edge: Drugs and the Consumption of Risk in Late Modernity, in S. Lyng (ed.), *Edgework: The Sociology of Risk Taking*. New York: Routledge, 227–45.

Robins, R. (2002). The Realness of Risk: Gene Technology in Germany. *Social Studies of Science*, 32 (1), 7–35.

Rogers, R. A. (1994). *Nature and the Crisis of Modernity*. Montreal: Black Rose Books.

Rorty, R. (1989). *Contingency, Irony and Solidarity*. Cambridge: Cambridge University Press.

Rosa, E. A. and T. Dietz (1998). Climate Change and Scientific Investigation. *International Sociology*, 13 (4), 421–55.

Rose, N. (1996). The Death of the Social? Re-figuring the Territory of Government. *Economy and Society*, 25 (3), 327–56.

Rose, N. (1999). *Powers of Freedom*. Cambridge: Cambridge University Press.

Rose, N. (2000). Government and Control. *British Journal of Criminology*, 40 (2), 321–39.

Rothstein, H., M. Huber and G. Gaskell (2006). A Theory of Risk Colonization: The Spiralling Regulatory Logics of Societal and Institutional Risk. *Economy and Society*, 35 (1), 91–112.

Sagan, S. D. (2004). Learning from Normal Accidents. *Organization and Environment*, 17 (1), 15–19.

Schudson, M. (1995). *The Power of News*. Cambridge, MA: Harvard University Press.

Schudson, M. (2003). *The Sociology of News*. New York: W. W. Norton.

Schulz, W. (1997). Changes of the Mass Media and the Public Sphere. *Javnost-The Public*, 4 (2), 57–69.

Schwarz, M. and M. Thompson (1990). *Divided We Stand*. Hemel Hempstead: Harvester Wheatsheaf.

Science and Society (2000). House of Lords Select Committee on Science and Technology Third Report. London: HMSO.

Scott, A. (1996). Risk Society or Angst Society?, in B. Adam, U. Beck and J. v. Loon (eds.), *The Risk Society and Beyond*. London: Sage, 33–46.

Seigneur, V. (2006). The Problems of Defining the Risks: The Case of Mountaineering. *Forum: Qualitative Social Research*, 7 (1), Art. 14.

Sennett, R. (1998). *The Corrosion of Character*. New York: W. W. Norton.

Shamir, R. (2005). Without Borders? Notes on Globalization as a Mobility Regime. *Sociological theory*, 23 (2), 197–217.

Shaw, M. (2005). *The New Western Way of War: Risk-Transfer War and Its Crisis in Iraq*. Cambridge: Polity Press.

Short, J. (1992). Defining, Explaining, and Managing Risk, in L. Clarke and J. Short (eds.), *Organizations, Uncertainties and Risk*. Boulder: Westview Press, 3–26.

Silverstone, R. (2007). *Media and Morality: On the Rise of the Mediapolis*. Cambridge: Polity Press.

Simmel, G. (1990). *The Philosophy of Money*. London: Routledge.

Simon, J. (2004). Taking Risks: Extreme Sports and the Embrace of Risk in Advanced Liberal Societies, in J. Simon and T. Baker (eds.), *Embracing Risk*. Chicago: Chicago University Press, 177–208.

Sismondo, S. (1993). Some Social Constructions. *Social Studies of Science*, 23, 515–53.

Slater, M. D. and K. A. Rasinski (2005). Media Exposure and Attention as Mediating Variables Affecting Social Risk Judgments. *Journal of Communication*, 55 (4), 810–27.

Slovic, P. (1987). Perception of Risk. *Science*, 236 (4799), 280–5.

Slovic, P., B. Fischhoff and S. Lichtenstein (1979). Rating the Risk. *Environment*, 21 (3), 14–20, 36–9.

Stallings, R. (1990). Media Discourse and the Social Construction of Risk. *Social Problems*, 37 (1), 80–95.

Stehr, N. (1994). *Knowledge Societies*. London: Sage.

Stocking, H. S. (1999). How Journalists Deal with Scientific Uncertainty, in S. M. Friedman, S. Dunwoody and C. L. Rogers (eds.), *Communicating Uncertainty*. Mahwah: Lawrence Erlbaum, 23–42.

Stove, D. C. (1973). *Probability and Hume's Inductive Scepticism*. Oxford: Clarendon Press.

Strydom, P. (2002). *Risk, Environment and Society*. Buckingham: Open University Press.

Sturgis, P. and N. Allum (2004). Science in Society: Re-evaluating the Deficit Model of Public Attitudes. *Public Understanding of Science*, 13 (1), 55–74.

Swan, E. J. (2000). *Building the Global Market*. The Hague: Kluwer Law.

Tait, J. and A. Bruce (2001). Globalisation and Transboundary Risk Regulation: Pesticides and Genetically Modified Crops. *Health, Risk and Society*, 3 (1), 99–112.

Tesh, S. N. (2000). *Uncertain Hazards*. Cornell: Cornell University Press.

Thompson, J. B. (1995). *Media and Modernity*. Cambridge: Polity Press.

Tichenor, P. J., G. A. Donohue, and C. N. Olien (1970). Mass Media Flow and Differential Growth in Knowledge. *The Public Opinion Quarterly*, 34 (2), 159–70.

Timotijevic, L. and J. Barnett (2006). Managing the Possible Health Risks of Mobile Telecommunications: Public Understandings of Precautionary Action and Advice. *Health, Risk and Society*, 8 (2), 143–64.

Tulloch, J. and D. Lupton (2001). Risk, the Mass Media and Personal Biography. *European Journal of Cultural Studies*, 4 (1), 5–27.

Turner, S. (1991). Social Constructionism and Social Theory. *Sociological Theory*, 9 (1), 22–33.

Velody, I. and R. Williams (1998). *The Politics of Constructionism*. London: Sage.

Waldrop, M. M. (1994). *Complexity – The Emerging Science at the Edge of Order and Chaos*. Harmondsworth: Penguin.

Webster, A. (2004). State of the Art: Risk, Science and Policy-Researching the Social Management of Uncertainty. *Policy Studies*, 25 (1), 5–18.

Wehling, P. (2001). Jenseits des Wissen? Wissenschaftliches Nichtwissen aus soziologischer Perspektive. *Zeitschrift für Soziologie*, 30 (6), 465–84.

White, R. (1999). *Putting Risk in Perspective: Black Teenage Lives in the Era of AIDS*. Landham: Rowman & Littlefield.

Wynne, B. (1989). Building Public Concerns into Risk Management, in J. Brown (ed.), *Environmental Threats: Perception, Analysis and Management*. London: Belhaven Press, 118–32.

Wynne, B. (1992). Uncertainty and Environmental Learning. *Global Environmental Change*, 2 (2), 111–27.

Wynne, B. (1996). May the Sheep Safely Graze?, in S. Lash, B. Szerszynski and B. Wynne (eds.), *Risk, Environment and Modernity*. London: Sage, 45–83.

Wynne, B. (2002). Risk and Environment as Legitimatory Discourses of Technology: Reflexivity Inside Out. *Current Sociology*, 50 (3), 459–77.

Yearly, S. (1992). Green Ambivalence about Science: Legal-Rational Authority and the Scientific Legitimation of a Social Movement. *British Journal of Sociology*, 43 (4), 511–32.

Yearly, S. (2005). *Making Sense of Science*. London: Sage.

Yesil, B. (2006). Watching Ourselves. *Cultural Studies*, 20 (4–5), 400–16.

Zaloom, C. (2006). *Out of the Pits*. Chicago: University of Chicago Press.

Zehr, S. C. (1999). Scientists' Representations of Uncertainty, in S. M. Friedman, S. Dunwoody and C. L. Rogers (eds.), *Communicating Uncertainty*. Mahwah: Lawrence Erlbaum, 3–22.

Zwick, D. (2005). Where the Action Is: Internet Stock Trading as Edgework. *Journal of Computer Mediated Communication*, 11 (1), Art. 2.

Index